JN422750

영어
하루에 3문장만
외우자!

영어회화에 꼭 필요한 **문법**과 **표현**이 한 곳에

영어 하루에 3문장만 외우자!

YOU ONLY NEED THREE SENTENCES A DAY TO BECOME A 영어짱

| Sarah Oh 지음 |

하루에 세 문장으로 영어회화에 꼭 필요한
문법 공부 끝 & 기본 표현 연습 끝!

맵시터

영어 하루에 3문장만 외우자

1판 1쇄 발행 2023년 8월 10일

지 은 이 | Sarah Oh
펴 낸 이 | 김정희
펴 낸 곳 | 맵씨터
등 록 | 제1994-9호
주 소 | 서울시 성동구 아차산로49, 404호
(성수동1가, 서울숲코오롱디지털타워3차)
전 화 | 02-464-7708
팩 스 | 02-499-0846
이 메 일 | hkm7708@daum.net
홈페이지 | http://hph.co.kr

ISBN 979-11-85923-35-2 03740

· 이 책의 내용은 저작권법에 따라 보호받고 있습니다.
· 잘못된 책은 구매처에서 바꾸어 드립니다.
· 책값은 뒤표지에 있습니다.

오류를 발견하셨다면 이메일이나 홈페이지를 통해 제보해주세요.
소중한 의견을 모아 더 좋은 책을 만들겠습니다.

머리말

언어는 '문법과 단어'로 구성되어 있습니다. 어떤 언어를 알기위해서는 문법과 단어를 알면 됩니다. 이 책은 Part 1 문법편과 Part 2 표현편으로 나뉘어 있습니다.

문법편은 어려운 설명, 용어는 될 수 있는 대로 없애고 회화에 꼭 필요한 모든 기본 문법규칙들을 문장 속에 담았습니다. 이미 잘 알고 있는 부분은 그냥 넘어가도 되지만 하루에 세 문장이니 부담 없이 문장들을 읽어가다 보면 문장구조에 점점 익숙해질 것입니다.

표현편에 있는 단어와 표현들은 잠깐 스치고 지나가는 유행어나 어느 한 세대에서만 쓰이는 혹은 평생 쓰지 않을 어려운 단어들이 아닌 누구나에게 필요하고 일상생활에서 자주 쓰이는 단어와 표현들, 하지만 막상 말로 하려면 실수가 많은 것 위주로 담았습니다. 더 쉽고 간단한 표현으로 대체가 가능한 표현들은 배제하려고 노력하였습니다.

Part 1 문법편은 요리법(recipe)입니다. 말 그대로 요리하는 방법을 터득하는 거죠. 즉 제대로 된 문장구조를 만들어 낼 수 있는 방법을 문법편에서 익힐 수 있습니다. Part 2 표현법은 재료입니다. 요리하는 방법은 아는데 재료가 없으면 아무 소용이 없겠죠. 문법 규칙들을 익힌 후에는 꾸준히 새로운 단어들을 익혀가는 것이 영어 공부의 정석입니다. 문법 규칙은 숫자가 정해져 있기 때문에 본인의 의지에 따라 터득하는 시간을 얼마든지 줄일 수 있지만 숫자가 정해져 있지 않은 단어와 표현들은 욕심을 내지 않고 매일 조금씩 꾸준히 연습하는 것이 답입니다.

부디 이 책이 영어의 일부분이 아닌 영어의 전체 그림을 보여드려 문법책, 단어책, 표현책, 회화책들을 다 따로 살 필요 없이 이 책 한권으로 일 년 후에 '영어짱'이 될 수 있으시기를 진심으로 바랍니다.

이 책을 너무나도 예쁘고 공부할 맛이 나게 잘 포장해주신 진나경 대리님 그리고 조정흠 부장님께 깊이 감사드립니다.

차례

PART 1 문법편 Day 001~100

부록

PART 2 표현편 Day 101~365

PART 1
문법편

THREE
sentences
a day

영어는 반복하면 복이 와요!^^

Day 001

명령문 (1)

■ 주어 You를 생략하고 동사원형(go, look, make)으로 시작

① Read out loud!

소리 내어 읽어!

② Practice English every day!

매일 영어 연습해!

③ Don't waste your time!

너의 시간을 낭비하지 마!

Day 002

명령문 (2)

■ 동사 외(형용사 · 명사)는 am, are, is의 원형인 Be로 시작

① Be confident!(형용사)

자신감을 가져!

② Be a pro!(명사)

프로가 돼!

③ Don't be discouraged!(형용사)

용기 잃지 마!

Day 003

Be동사 (1)

- ~이다 / ~에 있다
- 앞의 주어에 따라 am, is, are로 형태가 바뀜.
- I+am / You와 주어가 하나보다 많을 때+are

① I am confident.

난 자신 있어.

② I am not confident.

나는 자신이 없어.

③ Are you confident?

너 자신 있니?

Day 004

Be동사 (2)

■ He, She, It에 해당하는 단어+is

① He is my older brother and she is my younger sister.

그는 나의 오빠(형)이고 그녀는 나의 여동생이야.

☑ They are my siblings. 그들은 나의 형제(자매)야.

② We are not in the library.

우리 도서관에 없어.

③ Is it your friend's cat?

그것은 너의 친구의 고양이니?

Day 005

비인칭 주어 It

- 날씨, 날짜, 요일, 시간, 계절, 거리, 명암을 표현할 때 의미 없이 주어자리에 쓰임.

① It's Saturday, August 26th, 2023.

2023년 8월 26일 토요일이야.

② It's summer. It's not cold.

여름이야. 춥지 않아.

③ Is it two o'clock?

두시니?

Day 006

일반동사 (1)

- be동사(am, are, is)를 제외한 다른 동사들(go, study, read)
- 주어 뒤에 옴. 영어는 주어+동사.

① I like dogs. (=I'm a dog person.)

나는 개를 좋아해.

② I don't exercise every day.

나는 운동을 매일하지는 않아.

③ Do you have siblings?

너는 형제, 자매가 있니?

Day 007

일반동사 (2)

① We go to the same school.

우리는 같은 학교에 다녀.

② They wear uniforms.

그들은 교복(제복)을 입어.

③ Koreans eat rice every day.

한국 사람들은 매일 밥을 먹어.

Day 008

일반동사 - 3인칭 단수가 주어일 때 (1)

- 3인칭 단수(He, She, It에 해당하는 단어)가 주어일 때 동사 끝에 -s / -es / -ies를 붙임

  예) reads, goes, studies

  * have → has

① My mom likes flowers.

우리 엄마는 꽃을 좋아해.

② She doesn't know many singers.

그녀는 가수들을 많이 몰라.

③ Does your grandma enjoy watching TV?

너 네 할머니는 텔레비전 보는 걸 좋아하시니?

☑ 즐기니

Day 009

일반동사 - 3인칭 단수가 주어일 때 (2)

① He does his homework after school.

그는 방과 후에 숙제를 해.

② My aunt goes hiking every weekend.

우리 이모는 매주 산에 가.

③ The dog has beautiful eyes.

그 개는 아름다운 눈을 가지고 있어.

Day 010

시제 (1) - 현재

■ 시간(과거, 현재, 미래 등)에 따라 동사의 형태가 바뀜.

① I have(=eat) breakfast every day.

나는 매일 아침 식사를 해.

② He does his homework before dinner.

그는 저녁식사 전에 숙제를 해.

③ We study math at home.

우리는 집에서 수학공부를 해.

Day 011

시제 (2) - 현재진행

① I am eating breakfast now.

나 지금 아침 먹고 있어.

② She is doing her homework.

그녀는 지금 숙제하고 있어.

③ They are studying math.

그들은 수학 공부하고 있어.

Day 012

시제 (3) - 과거진행

- am, is → was
  are → were

① I was eating breakfast.

나 아침 먹고 있었어.

② My sister was doing her homework.

내 여동생은 숙제하고 있었어.

③ My friend and I were studying math.

내 친구와 나는 수학 공부를 하고 있었어.

Day 013

시제 (4) - 과거

- 동사 끝에 -d / -ed / -ied 가 붙음.

  예) liked played studied

- 불규칙 동사(see→ saw) 등은 이 책 속의 많은 문장에서 익히기.

① I ate breakfast.

나 아침 먹었어.

② They didn't do their homework.

그들은 숙제를 안했어.

③ Did you study math?

너 수학 공부했니?

Day 014

시제 (5) - 미래

① I will have breakfast.

나 아침 먹을 거야.

☑ I won't have breakfast. 나 아침 안 먹을 거야.

Will you have breakfast? 너 아침 먹을 거니?

② I am going to eat breakfast.

나 아침 먹을 거야.

☑ 미리 계획한 것을 말할 때

She is going to

They are going to

③ I am eating breakfast at grandma's tomorrow.

나 내일 할머니 댁에서 아침 먹어.

☑ 빠른 시일 내에 있을 확실한 계획일 때

Day 015

시제 (6) - 현재완료

① I have tried 번데기. (I've tried)

나 번데기 먹어 본 적 있어.

☑ I haven't tried 번데기(I've never tried). 난 번데기를 먹어 본적이 없어.

☑ Have you (ever) tried 번데기? 넌 번데기를 먹어 본적이 있니?

☑ He has tried 번데기. (He's tried) 그는 번데기를 먹어 본적이 있어.

② I have been to 부산.

나 부산에 가 본적 있어.

☑ Have you (ever) been to 부산? 너 부산에 가 본적 있니?

③ I have studied math.

나 여태까지 수학 공부했어.

Day 016

시제 (7) - 현재완료진행

① I've been studying.

나 지금까지 공부했어.

☑ She has been … ing (She's been … ing)

② I've been Practicing English.

나 여태까지 영어 연습했어.

③ I've been studying English hard.

나는 열심히 영어 공부를 해 왔어.

Day 017

시제 (8) - 과거완료

① When 칠득 got home I had already had lunch.

칠득이가 집에 왔을 땐 난 이미 점심을 다 먹었었어.

② when I got there 칠자 had gone home.

내가 거기에 도착했을 때 칠자는 집에 가고 없었어.

③ I didn't want to see the movie because I had already seen it.

나는 그 영화가 보고 싶지 않았어 왜냐하면 이미 그 영화를 봤었거든.

Day 018

시제 (9) - 과제완료진행

① When I met you at the bus stop yesterday I had been waiting for the bus for 20 minutes.

내가 어제 너를 버스정류장에서 만났을 때 나는 버스를 20분 기다리고 있었어.

② When it started raining we had been playing soccer for 30 minutes.

비가 오기 시작했을 때 우리는 축구를 30분 정도 하고 있었어.

③ My dad had been smoking for 20 years but he gave up last year.

우리 아빠는 20년 동안 담배를 피우셨었는데 작년에 끊으셨어.

Day 019

시제 (10) - 미래진행

① I'll be watching the soccer game by then.

나 그 시간에는 축구 보고 있을 거야.

② Tomorrow 10? My mom will be working.

내일 10시? 우리 엄마는 일하고 있을 거야.

③ I'll be having dinner around 7.

7시쯤이면 나 저녁 먹고 있을 거야.

Day 020

시제 (11) - 미래완료

① The soccer game will have finished by then.

그 시간에는 축구가 끝나 있을 거야.

② At 11? My mom will have finished her work.

11시? 우리 엄마 일이 끝나 있을 거야.

③ I'll have finished dinner around 8.

8시쯤이면 나 저녁 다 먹었을 거야.

Day 021

시제 (12) - 미래완료진행

① I'll have been studying here for two years next year.

내년이면 내가 여기서 공부한 지 이 년이 된다.

② My dad will have been working there for 30 years this September.

이번 9월이면 우리 아빠가 거기서 일한 지 30년이 될 거야.

③ I'll have been living here for 10 years next month.

다음 달이면 내가 여기에 산 지 10년이 될 거야.

Day 022

조동사 can/could (1)

■ 조동사+동사원형

① I can ride a bike.

나 자전거 탈 수 있어.

☑ I can not(can't)

② Can you solve this math problem?

너 이 수학문제 풀 수 있니?

② Can I have a hot chocolate, please?

코코아 주세요!

Day 023

조동사 can/could (2)

① Could you say that again, please?

그것을 다시 말씀해 주시겠어요?

② I was sick so I couldn't go there.

나 아파서 거기에 못 갔어.

= I wasn't able to go there. (못했다)

③ I could have gone there if I hadn't been sick.

내가 안 아팠으면 갈 수 있었을 텐데.

* could: · can의 과거형
  · 정중하게 말할 때
  · 가능성이 희박할 때
  · 제안할 때

Day 024

조동사 will/would (1)

① I will open the windows.

창문들 좀 열어야지.

☑ 할 거야/일 거야

② She won't be here soon.

그녀는 금방 안 올 거야.

☑ will not → won't

③ Will you do me a favor?

부탁 좀 들어줄래?

Day 025

조동사 will/would (2)

① Would you like some water?

물 좀 드실래요?

② If I were you, I wouldn't go there.

내가 너라면 난 거기에 안갈 것 같아.

③ I would have called you if I had known your number.

내가 너 연락처를 알았으면 전화를 했겠지.

Day 026

조동사 might=may (1)

① I might meet my friend today.

나 오늘 친구 만날지도 몰라.

☑ Might you … ?

② I might not take a bus. I might walk there.

나 버스 안탈지도 몰라. 거기에 걸어갈지도 몰라.

☑ might not → mightn't

③ It might have taken more time if we had driven a car.

운전을 했으면 시간이 더 걸렸을지도 몰라.

Day 027

조동사 might=may (2)

① We might as well walk home.

집에 걸어가는 수밖에.

② He may(=might) be wrong.

그가 틀릴 수도 있어.

③ Maybe, he is right.

그의 말이 맞을지도 몰라.

Day 028

조동사 should (1)

① I should exercise more.

난 운동을 더 해야 돼.

② It should be enough.

그것으로 충분할거야.

③ What should I order?

뭘 주문하지(할까)?

Day 029

조동사 should (2)

① Should I buy this one or that one?

이거 살까 아니면 저거 살까?

= Shall I … ?

② I should have done my homework first.

먼저 숙제부터할걸.

③ I shouldn't have eaten 라면 at night.

밤에 라면 먹지 말걸.

Day 030

조동사 must (1)

① We must stop at the red light.

빨간불에선 반드시 멈춰야해.

② You must not make any noise.

떠들면 안 돼.

☑ must not → mustn't

③ Must you make noise now?

지금 꼭 시끄럽게 해야 하니?

= Do you have to(need to) make noise?

Day 031

조동사 must (2)

① He must be playing a video game now.

그는 지금 비디오게임을 하고 있는 게 틀림없어.

② He must have studied hard.

그는 공부를 열심히 한 것이 틀림없어.

③ It must have been really hard.

힘들었겠다.

☑ It must've been fun. 재밌었겠다.

Day 032

조동사 have to (1)

① I have to do my homework.

나 숙제해야 해.

② I don't have to do the dishes but I want to.

내가 설거지를 하지 않아도 되지만 하고 싶어.

③ Do you have to go to the dentist?

너 오늘 치과에 가야 하니?

Day 033

조동사 have to (2)

① My friend has to take a test again.

내 친구는 다시 시험을 봐야해.

② You didn't have to go see the doctor again?

너 의사한테 다시 안 가 봐도 됐어?

☑ 안 해도 됐어

③ She had to go back to school.

그녀는 학교에 다시 가야했어.

Day 034

가주어 It (1)

- 예) 'To get up early is hard.'를 편의상 자리를 바꿔 주어를 뒤에 말함.
  (To get up early: 주어)

① It's hard to get up early.

일찍 일어나는 것은 힘들어.

② It's common for korean students to wear uniforms.

한국 학생들이 교복을 입는 것은 흔한 일이야.

③ It's amazing that a five year old boy speaks five languages.

5살짜리 꼬마가 5개 국어를 하다니 놀랍다.

Day 035

가주어 It (2)

① It's not helpful to blame others.

다른 사람들을 비난하는 것은 도움이 안 돼.

② Is it possible for us to memorize all of them?

우리가 그것들을 다 외우는 것이 가능할까?

③ It's no secret that I'm a genius.

내가 천재라는 것은 비밀이 아니야.

Day 036

There is (1)

■ '~이/가 있다'

① There is a bank.

은행이 있어.

② There are many apartment buildings in my neighborhood.

우리 동네에는 아파트들이 많이 있어.

③ There can't be any convenience store on this island.

이 섬에 편의점이 있을 리가 없어.

Day 037

There is (2)

① I think there should be more libraries.

나는 도서관이 더 있어야 한다고 생각해.

② There must be a convenience store somewhere.

어딘가에 편의점이 틀림없이 있을 거야.

③ A: There won't be any christmas events this year.
B: I heard there's going to be a christmas party next month.

A: 올해는 그 어떤 크리스마스 행사도 없을 거야.
B: 내가 듣기로는 다음 달에 크리스마스파티가 있을 거래.

☑ ~가 있을 거야

Day 038

비교급 (1)

- '형용사/부사+er than' ~보다 더~한
- 긴 단어(beautiful, fantastic 등)나 예외의 단어(fun, boring 등)는 more+[형용사/부사]+than

① I need a bigger box.

나 더 큰 상자가 필요해.

☑ big - bigger

② A: It's lighter.
B: I think that's heavier than this.

A: 이게 더 가벼워.
B: 그게 이거보다 더 무거운 거 같은데.

③ It's more difficult to come up with some Korean sentences than English ones.

영어문장들을 생각해내는 것보다 한국말 문장들을 생각해내는 게 더 어려워.

Day 039

비교급 (2)

① It's cheaper than that one.

이게 저것보다 더 싸.

② Your health is more important than your money.

돈보다 건강이 더 중요해.

③ It was more fun than a roller coaster.

그것은 롤러코스터보다 더 재밌었어.

☑ His English is way better than mine. 그의 영어실력이 나보다 훨씬 나아.

Day 040

최상급 (1)

- '(the) 형용사,부사+est': 가장, 제일~한
- 긴 단어나 예외의 단어는 '(the) most + 형용사, 부사'

① This saucepan is the biggest one.

이 냄비가 가장 큰 거야.

② This is the spiciest 떡볶이 I've ever eaten.

내가 지금까지 먹은 떡볶이 중에 이게 제일 매워.

③ I'm most tired when I solve math problems.

난 수학문제들을 풀 때 제일 피곤해.

Day 041

최상급 (2)

① I'm (the) tallest in my family.

내가 우리 집에서 키가 제일 커.

② What's the second biggest city in Korea?

한국에서 두 번째로 큰 도시가 어디야?

③ They were (the) most popular group in the world.

그들은 세계에서 가장 인기 있는 그룹이었어.

☑ 비교대상이 없을 땐 the 생략

Day 042

원급/as 관용구 (1)

- as [형용사/부사] as ~만큼~한

① It's as cold as yesterday.

어제만큼 추워.

② Was the test as hard as the last one?

그 시험이 지난번 시험만큼 어려웠니?

③ It's not as spicy as the one I ate with my friends.

이건 내 친구들이랑 먹은 것만큼은 안 매운데.

Day 043

원급/as 관용구 (2)

① My mom told me to come home as soon as possible.

우리엄마가 가능한 한 빨리 집에 오라고 하셨어.

② I try to wash my hands as often as I can.

나는 가능한 한 자주 손을 씻으려고 노력해.

③ It's my vacation. I can sleep as much as I want.

방학이야. 내가 자고 싶은 만큼 잘 수 있어.

Day 044

수동태 (1)

■ be+p.p(과거분사: eaten, seen, taken …) ~지다(~이 되다)

① What is this made of?

이것은 무엇으로 만들어진 거야?

② It is made of glass.

그건 유리로 만들어진 거야.

☑ be made [from/out of/with]

③ The building was built 200 years ago.

그 건물은 200년 전에 지어졌어.

Day 045

수동태 (2)

① He is known to lots of people.

그는 많은 사람들에게 알려져 있어.

② It is used for grinding something.

이것은 뭔가를 가는데 사용돼.

③ It's not designed for that purpose.

그건 그 목적으로 디자인이 된 게 아니야.

☑ It's designed to 동사원형

Day 046

의문사 (1) - What

① What are you doing this weekend?

이번 주말에 뭐해?

② Do you know what he is doing now?

너 그가 지금 뭐하고 있는지 아니?

③ What do you think I should do?

너 생각에는 내가 어떻게 해야 할 것 같아?

☑ What if 칠자 doesn't like pink?
만약에 칠자가 분홍색을 싫어하면 어떡하지?

Day 047

의문사 (2) - When

① When does the movie start?

그 영화 언제 시작해?

② Do you know when it starts?

그거 언제 시작하는지 아니?

③ When do you think he'll come?

너 생각에는 그가 언제 올 거 같으니?

Day 048

의문사 (3) - Where

① Where are you now?

너 지금 어디야?

② Where have you been?

어디 갔다 왔어?

③ Where do you think I should go?

너 생각에는 내가 어디를 가면 좋겠니?

Day 049

의문사 (4) - Who

① Who is she?

그녀는 누구야?

② Who made this?

이거 누가 만들었어?

③ Who do you think will be there?

거기에 누가 있을 거 같니?

Day 050

의문사 (5) - Why

① Why is it important?

그게 왜 중요해?

② Why do you think he is so popular?

너는 그가 왜 그렇게 인기가 있다고 생각하니?

③ Do you know why he is so popular?

너는 그가 왜 그렇게 인기가 있는지 아니?

☑ Why not go there by yourself? 거기에 혼자가지 그러니?

Day 051

의문사 (6) - How

① How is your grandma?

너 네 할머니는 잘 계시니?

② How many people are there in your family?

너네는 가족이 몇 명이야?

③ How often do you go to a hair salon?

너는 얼마나 자주 미용실에 가니?

Day 052

의문사 (7) - How

① How old is this building?

이 건물은 얼마나 오래됐어?

② How long does it take to get there?

거기 가는데 얼마나 걸려?

③ How about going to the library?

도서관에 가는 건 어때?

☑ How about pizza?
How about eating pizza?
How about we eat pizza?

Day 053

의문사 (8) - Which

① Which one do you like better, 짜장 or 짬뽕?

너는 짜장, 짬뽕 중에 어느 것이 더 좋아?

② Which of your siblings do you feel closer to?

너 네 형제 중에 누구랑 더 친해?

③ I don't know which one is which.

어느 게 어느 건지 모르겠어.

Day 054

의문사 (9) - Whose

① Whose umbrella is this?

이 우산 누구 거야?

② Do you know whose umbrella it is?

너 이거 누구 우산인지 아니?

③ I don't know whose one it is.

누구 건지 모르겠는데.

Day 055

빈도부사 (1)

① I always drink some water as soon as I get up.

나는 항상 일어나자마자 물을 마셔.

☑ I'm always happy. (be동사 뒤에)

② She usually goes to church on Sunday.

그녀는 일요일엔 보통 교회에 가.

③ He often plays video games after school.

그는 방과 후에 자주 비디오게임을 해.

Day 056

빈도부사 (2)

① Sometimes, I feel down for no reason.

가끔 이유 없이 우울해질 때가 있어.

② I rarely watch TV. I watch Youtube.

나는 텔레비전은 거의 안 봐. 난 유투브를 봐.

= hardly/barely

③ I sometimes do the dishes but I never vaccum.

나는 가끔 설거지는 하지만 청소기는 안 돌려.

☑ 절대 아니다/절대 ~하지 않다

Day 057

전치사 (1) - about

■ 전치사+명사

① Please, tell me about your country!

당신의 나라에 대해서 말해주세요!

② What do you like about winter?

너는 겨울의(대한) 어떤 점이 좋니?

③ This story is about a girl.

이 이야기는 한 소녀에 관한 거야.

* 전치사 뒤에 올 수 있는 명사 종류: 명사, 대명사, 동명사, w의문사

명사: desk | 대명사: that | 동명사: eating

w의문사: who, what, which, whom, whose, where, when, why, how, whether

Day 058

전치사 (2) - at

① I got up at seven today.

나 오늘 일곱 시에 일어났어.

② I had lunch at a restaurant with my family.

나는 가족들과 식당에서 점심 먹었어.

③ I don't go out at night.

나는 밤에 안 나가.

Day 059

전치사 (3) - in

① I was born in 2011.

나는 2011년에 태어났어.

② There are many national holidays in May in Korea.

한국에는 5월에 많은 공휴일이 있어.

③ My sister's birthday is in three days.

삼일 후면 내 동생 생일이야.

☑ in: ~이면 / ~ 만에 / ~ 후에, 뒤에

Day 060

전치사 (4) - with/without

① I usually have dinner with my family.

나는 보통 가족과 저녁을 먹어.

② Should I eat this with chopsticks or a fork?

이거 젓가락으로 먹어야해 아니면 포크로 먹어야해?

③ 깍두기 is made with radish.

깍두기는 무로 만들어져.

☑ 백김치 is made without chili powder. 백김치는 고춧가루 없이 만들어져.

Day 061

전치사 (5) - from/to

① I'm from South Korea.

나는 한국(남한)에서 왔어.

② Rainy season is from mid June to late July.

장마는 6월 중순부터 7월 말까지야.

☑ 7월 초 - early July

③ My family and I went on a trip to 제주도.

가족들과 제주도로 여행 갔었어.

Day 062

전치사 (6) - on

① Let's meet on Monday

우리 월요일에 만나자!

② I saw it on TV.

나 그거 텔레비전에서 봤어.

③ I left my cell phone on the table.

나 식탁 위에 핸드폰을 두고 왔어.

Day 063

전치사 (7) - under

① There's something under the desk.

책상 밑에 뭐가 있어.

② A: How old are you? ten?
B: Under.

A: 너 몇 살이야? 열 살?
B: 그것보다 아래.

③ The building is under construction.

그 건물은 공사 중이야.

Day 064

전치사 (8) - above/below

① There is a picture above the drawer.

서랍 위에 그림이 하나있어.

☑ There is a drawer below the picture. 그림 밑에 서랍이 있어.

② A: I got a 70 in my math test.
B: Is it above average or below?

A: 나 수학 시험 70점 맞았어.
B: 그거 평균 이상이야 이하야?

③ The temperature is below zero.

오늘 기온이 영하야.

Day 065

전치사 (9) - for

① I made this for my mom.

나 이거 엄마를 위해 만들었어.

② She got scolded for eating in class.

그녀는 수업시간에 먹어서 혼났어.

☑ ~ 때문에, 이유로

③ His korean is excellent for a person who has been in Korea for two years.

한국에 이년 산 사람 치고는 그는 한국말을 정말 잘해.

Day 066

전치사 (10) - by/until

① I should finish this by Friday so I'll be busy until then.

나 금요일 전까지 이거 끝내야 해 그래서 그때까지 바쁠 거야.

접속사 Until I finish

② The book was written by her.

그 책은 그녀에 의해 쓰였다.

③ Do you go to school by bus?

너는 버스 타고 학교에 가니?

☑ by+교통수단: ~로(을/를 타고)

Day 067

전치사 (11) - before

① What do you usually do before school?

너는 학교 가기 전에 보통 뭐니?

② Some people brush their teeth before having breakfast.

어떤 사람들은 아침식사 전에 이를 닦아.

③ 접속사 I eat some snacks before I do my homework.

나는 숙제하기 전에 간식을 좀 먹어.

Day 068

전치사 (11) - after

① My sister's birthday is just after my birthday.

내 동생 생일은 내 생일 바로 다음이야.

② I promise I'll clean up here after watching this.

내가 이거 보고난 후에 여기 치울게, 약속해.

③ 접속사 What did you do after you talked to your friend on the phone?

친구랑 통화한 후에 뭐했어?

Day 069

전치사 (12) - between

① What's your favorite, between 불고기, 잡채, 비빔밥?

너는 불고기, 잡채, 비빔밥 중에 뭐가 제일 좋니?

② Where would you like to travel, between 프랑스, 아프리카, 스페인?

너는 프랑스, 아프리카, 스페인 중에 어디를 여행하고 싶어?

③ A: Do you know where the bank is?
B: It's between the convenience store and the bakery.

은행이 어디에 있는지 아니?
그 편의점하고 제과점 사이에 있어.

Day 070

전치사 (13) - among

① What's your favorite food among many Korean dishes?

많은 한국 음식들 중에 네가 가장 좋아하는 음식은 뭐야?

② Are they popular among your friends?

너의 친구들 사이에서 그들은 인기가 있니?

③ Among all the movies I've seen, this is the best.

내가 지금까지 본 모든 영화들 중에, 이게 최고야.

Day 071

전치사 (14) -
next to/in front of/behind/across from

① I was sitting next to a very famous singer on the subway today.

나 오늘 전철에서 되게 유명한 가수 옆에 앉아있었어.

② Is it in front of your place or behind?

그게 너의 집 앞에 있니 아니면 뒤에 있니?

③ There is a stationery store across from the park.

그 공원 건너편에 문구점이 있어.

Day 072

전치사 (15) - like

① Look at all the lights! It's like Christmas.

저 전등들 좀 봐! 크리스마스 같아.

② You're like my brother. He is also a huge fan of soccer.

너 우리 형 같다. 우리 형도 축구 엄청 좋아하거든.

③ I enjoy fruit like watermelon, peaches, and plums.

나는 수박, 복숭아, 자두 같은 과일들을 즐겨먹어.

Day 073

전치사 (16) - into

① When I walked into the room, I saw a cake on the table.

내가 방안에 들어갔을 때 식탁 위의 케이크를 봤어.

② Crack the egg into the bowl.

그 볼 안에 달걀을 깨서 넣어.

③ Can you translate this into Korean?

이거 한국말로 번역할 수 있니?

Day 074

전치사 (17) - out of

① Nine out of ten people have seen the movie.

10명 중에 9명은 그 영화를 봤어.

② Can you take it out of the bag, please?

그것 좀 가방에서 꺼내줄래?

☑ 가방 안에서 밖으로

③ Going somewhere out of Korea was out of the question during covid.

코로나 기간 동안 국외(한국 밖으로)로 나가는 건 불가능한 일이었어.

Day 075

전치사 (18) - of

① The capital of Korea is Seoul.

한국의 수도는 서울이야.

② One of my friends got hurt while playing basketball.

내 친구중의 한 명이 농구를 하다가 다쳤어.

③ Of all the places, why do you want to go to Alaska?

많은 곳 중에서 왜 알라스카에 가고 싶니?

Day 076

전치사 (19) - except

① I like all Korean food **except**(for) fermented skate.

나는 삭힌 홍어 **빼고** 한국 음식은 다 좋아해.

② I go to the park every day **except** when I don't feel good.

나는 몸이 안 좋을 때 **빼고는** 공원에 매일 가.

③ 접속사 The movie was okay **except** there weren't any actors I like.

내가 좋아하는 배우들이 없었던 것을 **제외하고는** 그 영화는 나쁘지 않았어.

Day 077

전치사 (20) - instead

① Is it okay to meet on Friday instead of Saturday?

토요일 대신 금요일에 만나도 될까?

② 부사 I didn't meet my friend, instead, I went to my grandma's place.

나 친구 안 만나고 대신 할머니 댁에 갔었어.

③ 부사 A: Let's take a taxi!
B: How about the subway instead?

A: 우리 택시 타자!
B: 대신 전철은 어때?

Day 078

전치사 (21) - around

① I usually get up around seven but I got up a bit late this morning.

나는 보통 7시쯤에 일어나는데 오늘아침에는 조금 늦게 일어났어.

② Do you live around here?

이 근처에 사니?

③ I'm going to travel around the world.

나는 세계 일주를 할 거야.

☑ 주위를 / 이곳저곳을

Day 079

전치사 (22) - during

① It's hot and humid during the summer in Korea.

한국은 여름 (동안)에는 덥고 습해.

② I've been to the bathroom during recess.

쉬는 시간동안 화장실에 갔다 왔어.

③ We swam during the day and played games at night.

우리는 낮 동안 수영하고 밤에는 게임을 했어.

Day 080

전치사 (23) - including

① I can play several musical instruments including ukulele.

나는 우쿨렐레를 포함해서 몇 가지의 악기를 연주할 수 있어.

② I've tried all kinds of 떡볶이 including 궁중떡볶이.

나는 모든 종류의 떡볶이를 다 먹어봤어 궁중떡볶이를 포함해서.

③ There are four people in my family including myself.

우리 가족은 나를 포함해서 네 명이야.

Day 081

전치사 (24) - along

① Did you ever ride a bike along the Han river?

너 한강을 따라 자전거를 타 본적이 있니?

② There are lots of shops and restaurants along the beach.

해변을 따라 많은 가게들과 식당들이 있어.

③ Can I tag along?

따라가도 돼?

Day 082

전치사 (25) - other than

- = aside from / apart from / besides

① I watched some youtube videos, other than that … nothing special.

나는 유트브 좀 봤고 그것 말고는 … 별거 없어.

② Other than 순대, what did you eat?

순대 말고 또 뭐 먹었어?

③ Aside from the weather, everything was perfect.

날씨 말고는 모든 게 완벽했어.

Day 083

전치사 (26) - through

① His dog can jump and go through the ring.

그의 개는 점프해서 그 링을 통과할 수 있어.

② We went through a tunnel

우리는 터널을 통과했어.

③ Be careful, when you walk through the door.

그 문을 통과할 때 조심해.

Day 084

관계대명사

- 앞의 명사를 부연 설명: 사람(who/that), 사람 외(which/that)

① This is the bread which(=that) I wanted to eat.

이게 내가 먹고 싶었던 빵이야.

☑ 어떤 빵이냐 하면

☑ This is (명사×) what I wanted to eat. 이게 내가 먹고 싶었던 거야.

② That's the person who(=that) I saw on TV.

저 사람은 내가 텔레비전에서 본 사람이야.

☑ 어떤 사람이냐 하면

③ There's a boy whose father is a famous movie star in my class.

우리 반에 아빠가 유명한 영화배우인 남자아이가 있어.

☑ 누구의(그 소년의)

* that 뒤에 주어+동사가 오면 생략 가능
예) This is the bread I wanted to eat.

Day 085

관계부사

■ 장소, 시간, 이유, 방법을 부연 설명

① This is the place where(=that) I learned 태권도 when I was little.

여기가 내가 어렸을 때 태권도를 배웠던 곳이야.

* where: '장소'외에도 더 폭넓게 쓰임.
  예) … time where / … situation where

② There were times when(=that) I wanted to give up but I didn't.

포기하고 싶었던 때도 있었지만 난 그러지 않았어.

③ That's the reason why(=that) I became a 영어짱.

그게 내가 영어짱이 된 이유야.

④ This is (명사×) how I became a 영어짱.

이게 내가 영어짱이 된 방법이야.

☑ This is the way (that) I became a 영어짱.

Day 086

접속사 (1)

■ 접속사 + 단어 / 구 / 절 / 문장

① We might eat out or order(in) some delivery food today.

우리 오늘 외식하거나 아니면 배달 음식을 시켜 먹을지도 몰라.

② You'd better eat breakfast or else you'll be hungry at school.

아침밥을 먹는 게 좋을 걸 그렇지 않으면 너 학교에서 배고플 거야.

③ I turned down the TV so that I could hear what he said.

나는 텔레비전 소리를 줄였어 그래서 그가 뭐라고 하는지 들을 수 있게.

Day 087

접속사 (2)

① I eat sweets when I get stressed out.

나는 스트레스를 받을 때 단 것을 먹어.

② I did my homework while my mom was making dinner.

우리 엄마가 저녁준비 하는 동안 나는 숙제했어.

☑ She is quiet and reserved while her brother is outgoing.
그녀의 오빠는 활달한 반면 그녀는 조용하고 내성적이야.

③ I'll just stay at home if it rains.

만약에 비가 오면 그냥 집에 있을 거야.

☑ Could you ask 칠득 if (Whether) he eats meat?
칠득이한테 고기 먹는지 물어봐 줄래?

Day 088

접속사 (3)

① We couldn't go camping because it was raining.

우리 비 때문에 캠핑 못갔어.

전치사 We couldn't go camping because of rain.
우리 비가 와서 캠핑 못갔어.

② As it was getting cold, we decided to go home.

점점 추워져서 우리는 집에 가기로 했어.

☑ 때문에(이유)

③ 전치사 As a student, I should study hard.

학생으로서, 난 열심히 공부해야해.

Day 089

접속사 (4)

① It's been a while since I went to an amusement park.

놀이공원에 갔다 온 지 꽤 됐어.

☑ ~이후로

☑ It's been a while since+과거시제/현재완료

② Since we're in 부산 why don't we try 부산오뎅?

우리 부산에 왔으니까 부산오뎅이나 먹을까?

③ 전치사 I haven't eaten anything since last night.

나 어제 밤부터 아무것도 안 먹었어.

☑ ~이후로

Day 090

접속사 (5)

① I played soccer even though it was raining.

비가 왔지만 축구를 했어.

☑ ~임에도 불구하고

② Even if it rains, I'll play soccer.

만약에 비가와도 난 축구를 할 거야.

☑ 만약에 ~일지라도

③ You don't have to go there unless you really want to.

네가 정말 원하지 않는다면 거기에 안 가도 돼.

Day 091

접속사 (6)

① Convenience stores are everywhere in Korea. You can see them wherever you go.

한국에는 편의점이 어디에나 있어. 네가 어디를 가든 편의점들을 볼 수 있을 거야.

☑ 어디든지

② Whenever(=every time) I go there, I always eat ice cream.

난 거기에 갈 때마다 항상 아이스크림을 먹어.

③ Whatever we do and say, we shouldn't forget that we all reap what we sow."

우리가 무엇을 하고 말하든 우리가 뿌린 것을 거두며 살아간다는 것을 우리는 잊으면 안 돼.

☑ 무엇이든

Day 092

접속사 (7)

① Once you start reading the book, you can't put it down.

한번(일단) 그 책을 읽기 시작하면 내려놓을 수가 없어.

② The moment I wake up, I say "Hello, today!"

나는 잠에서 깨어나는 순간 "안녕, 오늘아"라고 말해.

③ In order to stay healthy, what should we do?

건강을 유지하기위해서 우리는 무엇을 해야 할까?

Day 093

접속사 (8)

① I like both summer and winter.

나는 여름과 겨울 둘 다 좋아.

② A: Do you have any plans for the weekend?
B: I don't have any particular plans. I can either go to the library or meet some friends.

A: 주말에 무슨 계획이라도 있니?
B: 계획은 특별히 없어. 도서관에 갈수도 있고 혹은 친구들을 만날 수도 있고.

☑ either A or B: A 혹은 B

③ I like neither summer nor winter. summer is too hot and winter is too cold.

나는 여름도 싫고 겨울도 싫어. 여름은 너무 덥고 겨울은 너무 춥잖아.

= I don't like either of them. 둘 다 싫어.

Day 094

to

① I went to the store to get some milk

나 우유 사러 가게에 갔었어.

☑ 하기 위해

② I need something to read.

나 뭔가 읽을게 필요해.

☑ ~할

③ Is this pot big enough to cook all these noodles?

이 국수 다 끓이기에 이 냄비가 충분히 큰가?

☑ ~하기에, 할 정도로

Day 095

-ing

① I was in the park **looking** at some ants.

개미들을 **보면서** 공원에 있었어.

② I was watching TV **eating** some snacks.

나는 간식을 좀 **먹으면서** 텔레비전을 보고 있었어.

③ I was on the way home **talking** to my friends.

친구들하고 **얘기하면서** 집에 오는 길이었어.

Day 096

-ed

① This is the chair designed by my uncle.

이게 우리 삼촌이 디자인한 의자야.

☑ 디자인된

② There is a building built in 1600 in that city.

1600년에 지어진 건물이 그 도시에 있어.

③ I ate 김치 made by a foreigner.

외국인이 만든 김치를 먹었어.

☑ 만들어진

Day 097

긴 주어 (1)

① The first thing (that) I do in the morning is make my bed.

내가 아침에 제일 먼저 하는 것은 이불(침대)정리하는 거야.

② What happened in school today was one of my classmates cried because her team lost the dodge ball game.

오늘 학교에서 무슨 일이 있었냐하면 우리 반에 한명이 걔네 팀이 피구게임에서 졌다고 울었어.

③ The most popular Korean food among foreigners is Bulgogi.

외국인들 사이에서 가장 인기 있는 한국음식은 불고기야.

Day 098

긴 주어 (2)

① The reason (that) lots of people can't speak English well is they rarely speak in English.

많은 사람들이 영어를 잘 못하는 이유는 영어로 말을 거의 하지 않기 때문이야.

② The best way to improve your English skills is you should speak English as much as possible.

너의 영어실력을 향상시킬 수 있는 가장 좋은 방법은 가능한 한 영어로 많이 말을 하는 거야.

③ What I want to say is "you can do it!"

내가 말하고 싶은 것은 이거야 "너는 할 수 있어!"

Day 099

도치 (1)

- 주로 강조를 위한 어순의 바뀜
- 사용하기가 어려우면 안 써도 되지만 알아 놓으면 듣기에 도움이 됨.

① Here comes [the bus/the train/Jone …]!

[버스/기차/존] 온다!

= The bus is coming.

☑ There goes the bus! 버스 간다!

Here it comes / There it goes

② A: I am tired.
B: So am I. (=Me too.)

A: 나 피곤해.
B: 나도.

☑ so do I / so does he / neither do I

③ Never have I been so surprised.

내가 그렇게 놀란 적이 한 번도 없었어.

☑ I've never been so surprised.

Day 100

도치 (2)

① Not until you've finished your homework, can you watch TV.

너 숙제 끝내기 전까지는 텔레비전 못 봐.

→You can't watch TV until you have finished your homework.

② Not only does he speak English but also French.

그는 영어뿐만이 아니라 프랑스어도 할 수 있어.

→ He speaks not only English but also French.

③ Little did I know how much effort and time I needed to be a 영어짱.

영어짱이 되기 위해 얼마나 많은 노력과 시간이 필요한지 몰랐어.

→ I didn't know how much effort and time I needed to be a 영어짱.

부록 1

-ly로 끝나는 부사

01 That's exactly what I want to say.
그게 바로(정확하게) 내가 하고 싶은 말이야.

02 I'll definitely go there.
나는 거기에 꼭(당연히) 갈 거야.

03 I totally forgot.
나 완전히 잊어버렸어.

04 I like 떡볶이, especially 궁중떡볶이.
나는 떡볶이를 좋아해 특히 궁중떡볶이.

05 I just saw him briefly before heading to 부산.
부산에 가기 전에 그를 잠깐 봤어.

06 I fell down but luckily, I didn't get hurt.
나 넘어졌는데 다행히 다치지는 않았어.

07 He probably thought it was his.
그는 아마도 그것이 자기 것이라고 생각했나봐.

08 Seriously? You're not serious, are you?
진심이야? 너 진심 아니지, 그치?

09 The test was relatively easy.
그 시험은 비교적 쉬웠어.

10 You're absolutely right!

네 말이 완전 맞아!

11 I go there occasionally but I want to go there more frequently.

나는 거기에 가끔 가 하지만 더 자주 가고 싶어.

12 There are mainly Asians there.

거기에는 주로 아시아인들이 있어.

13 It's terribly hard for young people to get a job nowadays.

젊은이들이 직장을 구하는 것이 정말(부정적) 쉽지가 않아 요즘엔.

14 It was incredibly beautiful. I couldn't take my eyes off.

그것은 믿기지 않을 정도로 아름다웠어. 눈을 뗄 수가 없더라.

15 I wasn't able to understand it throughly.

나는 그것을 완벽히 이해하지는 못했어.

16 The work is extremely hard both emotionally and physically.

그 일은 감정적으로나 육체적으로 굉장히 힘든 일이야.

17 Fortunately, I was able to take the last train.

다행히 난 마지막 기차를 탈수 있었어.

18 Unfortunately, I wasn't able to go there.

불행히도 난 거기에 못 갔어.

19 I accidently push the power button.

내가 실수로 전원 버튼을 눌렀어.

20 Basically, you don't need to prepare anything.

기본적으로 너는 준비할 게 아무것도 없어.

21 Technically, You're not supposed to eat here.

엄밀히 말하면 너는 여기서 먹을 수 없어.

22 I'm currently between jobs.

나는 지금은(현재는) 직업이 없어.

23 I can easily get up at five in the morning.

나는 쉽게 아침 다섯 시에 일어날 수 있어.

24 Hopefully, the weather will be nice.

날씨가 좋았으면 좋겠다. (바라건대)

25 I hardly (rarely, barely) watch TV.

나는 TV를 거의 안 봐.

26 Obviously, he doesn't know about it.

명백히 그는 그것에 대해서 모르고 있어.

27 Apparently, he doesn't know about it.

보아하니, 그는 그것에 대해 모르는 것 같아.

28 Literally? or figuratively?

말 그대로 아니면 비유적으로?

29 The taste is slightly different.

맛이 조금 다른데.

30 Once it becomes a habit, you'll automatically wake up on time.

습관이 되면, 자동으로 제 시간에 일어나게 될 거야.

31 I got the answer immediately.

답을 바로(즉시) 받았어.

32 If you closely look at it, you'll be able to see it.

네가 그것을 가까이서 보면 보일거야.

33 It was originally my room but now it's my brother's.

그것은 원래 내방이었는데 지금은 내 동생이 써.

34 Korea has changed drastically for the past few years.

한국은 지난 몇 년간 확 바뀌었어.

35 My English has changed gradually not drastically.

나의 영어는 갑자기가 아니라 서서히 바뀌었어.

36 I particularly like this.

나는 특히 이게 마음에 들어.

37 Please, tell me specifically!

구체적으로 말해주세요!

38 It's entirely up to you!

그건 완전히 너한테 달렸어.

39 I certainly remember what you said.

난 당연히 네가 뭐라고 했는지 기억해.

40 Ironically, even though tomatoes are his least favorite, he likes tomato juice.

이상하게도 그가 가장 싫어하는 게 토마토인데 그는 토마토 주스는 좋아해.

41 He clearly didn't understand what was going on.

그는 무슨 일이 일어나고 있는지 분명히 몰랐어.

42 Personally, I prefer reading paper books to e-books.

개인적으로는 전자책보다는 종이책을 읽는 것을 더 좋아해.

43 Your English will improve Slowly but surely.

너의 영어는 더디지만 확실히 향상이 될 거야.

44 He is undoubtedly one of the richest men in the world.

그는 의심할 여지 없이 세계에서 가장 부자 중에 한 명이야.

45 It was largely because of the weather.(=mostly)

날씨가 주된 원인이었지.

46 Do it properly!

제대로 해!

47 Actually, I had a big lunch so I'm not hungry.

사실, 점심을 거하게 먹어서 배가 안 고파.

48 We normally go there by bus.

우리는 보통 버스로 거기에 가.

49 The weather is generally mild and gentle there.

거기는 보통(일반적으로) 온화하고 따뜻한 날씨에요.

50 Finally, I've finished 문법편. :)

드디어 문법편 끝났다.^^

부록 2

that 활용

01 Look at that!

» 약간 거리가 있는 것을 가리킬 때

02 That bag is mine.

» 명사와 같이 쓰여 형용사 역할을 할 때: 저 가방

03 Would you like some tea? That sounds good!

» 앞 문장 전체를 받을 때

04 Did you get that job?

» 언급했던 말에 대해서 얘기할 때

05 That's amazing!

» 형용사와 같이 쓰여 상대방의 말에 반응을 보일 때

06 It's not that cold./Is it that good?

» 형용사, 부사와 같이 쓰여 '그렇게, 그 정도'의 뜻

07 Did you see the pen that I bought yesterday?

» 앞에 말한 명사를 구체적으로 설명할 때

08 The man that is standing by the door is my friend.

» 앞에 말한 명사(사람)을 구체적으로 설명할 때

09 This is the place that I met her.

» 앞에 말한 장소를 구체적으로 설명할 때

10 That's the reason that I don't like the place.

» 앞에 말한 이유를 구체적으로 설명할 때

11 There were times that I didn't want to practice English.

» 앞에 말한 시간을 구체적으로 설명할 때

12 This is the way that I make 떡볶이.

» 앞에 말한 방법을 구체적으로 설명할 때

13 That he is a good person is truth.

» 주어역할을 할 때 '인 것'으로 해석

14 The fact is that I like them.

» 보어역할을 할 때

15 I know that he is a good person.

» 목적어역할을 할 때

16 I am happy that you're here today.

» 감정이나 느낌을 나타내는 형용사 뒤에서 '해서'로 해석

17 I was so tired that I couldn't do my homework.

» so ~ that: 너무 ~해서 ~하다

18 I studied hard so that I could get good grades.

» so that: ~하기 위해서

19 I like her that she did all the things for her friend.

» because의 의미로 쓰일 때

20 It was me that did the dishes yesterday.

» It ~ that 강조구문: ~한 것은 ~이다

21 **This summer was cooler than that of last year.**

» 'that of' 명사를 반복할 때

22 **I know 칠득 and 영철: this I met in high school and that I met in college.**

» 전자, 후자를 얘기할 때 '전자'를 나타냄

23 **Are you mad that you should do such a thing?**

» 주어+should와 같이 쓰여 '~하다니'의 뜻

PART 2
표현편

THREE
sentences
a day

영어는 사탕이 아니야. 까먹지 마!

Day 101

① **all the time**

You're looking at your cell phone all the time.

너는 항상 휴대폰을 보고 있잖아.

② **ago**

A: I want to eat something.

B: What? You had dinner ten minutes ago.

A: 나 뭔가 먹고 싶어.

B: 뭐? 너 10분전에 저녁 먹었잖아.

☑ You ate dinner before doing your home work.
너 숙제하기 전에 저녁식사 했잖아.

③ **already**

I've already had lunch. You go ahead!

나 이미 점심 먹었어. 너나 어서 먹어.

☑ already: 이미, 벌써 / 어서, 빨리

- Do it already! 어서 해! (빨리 좀 해) (*독촉할 때)

Day 102

① **lots of**

I used to read lots of comics when I was little.

나는 어렸을 때 만화책을 많이 읽었었어.

☑ lots of comics = a lot of comics = comics a lot.

② **a few**

A: Were there many people there?

B: A few.

A: 거기에 사람들이 많았니?

B: 좀 있었어.

↔ few 거의 없는

③ **a little**

A: Are you tired?

B: A little (bit).

A: 너 피곤하니?

B: 조금 피곤해.

↔ We have little time. 시간이 별로 없다.

Day 103

① **ask**

Can I ask you a question?

질문을 하나해도 될까요?

☑ ask: 물어보다/부탁하다

- I'll ask my mom to make 떡볶이. 엄마한테 떡볶이 만들어 달라고 해야지.

☑ [ask for+st / ask+w의문사 / ask if …]

② **as well**(=too)

You lived in 서울?I lived there as well.

너 서울에 살았었니? 나도 거기에 살았었어.

③ **as usual**(=as always)

I took some vitamin supplements after a meal as usual.

밥 먹고 여느 때처럼 비타민 보충제를 좀 먹었어.

Day 104

① **all day long**

What did you do all day long?

너 하루 종일 뭐했니?

② **away**

It is two weeks away to start school.

개학이 2주 남았어.

☑ away: 여기부터 ~만큼 떨어져있다

= It's in two weeks. 2주 후야.

③ **aim**

I'm aiming to lose 1kg a week.

나 한주에 1킬로그램씩 살을 뺄 거야.

☑ aim [for/at]: 겨냥하다, 목표로 하다

Day 105

① **as a result**

I didn't study at all. As a result, I got bad grades.

나 공부 전혀 안했어. 그 결과로, 난 나쁜 성적을 받았지.

② **at least**

I drink at least five glasses of water a day.

나는 하루에 적어도 다섯 잔의 물을 마셔.

③ **allow sb to**

My mom doesn't allow me to eat junk food but my dad lets me eat whatever I want.

우리엄마는 나 불량식품 못 먹게 하시는데 우리아빠는 내가 먹고 싶은 거 다 먹게 허락하셔.

☑ allow sb to: 허락하다 / ~하게하다

Day 106

① **at the time**

I guess I was too young at the time.

그때는 내가 너무 어렸지.

② **are you sure**

Are you sure you don't want to have dinner?

너 진짜 저녁 안 먹을 거야?

☑ are you sure: 확실하니?

③ **a must**

Your passport is a must when you go abroad.

해외에 갈 때 여권은 필수야.

Day 107

① not any more

I can't eat any more. I'm full.

나 더 이상은 못 먹어. 배불러.

② all I did

All I did was eat and sleep during 추석.

추석 연휴동안 내가 한 거라곤 먹고 잔 것뿐이야.

☑ All I need / All I want / All he does….

③ accidentally

I accidentally sent my teacher a message which was supposed to go to my friend.

내가 친구에게 보낼 문자를 실수로 우리 선생님한테 보냈어.

Day 108

① **and whatnot**(=and so on, and so forth)

We can enjoy fresh seafood, beautiful nature and whatnot.

우리는 신선한 해산물에 아름다운 경치 등등을 즐길 수 있어.

② **at the latest**

We should get there by seven at the latest.

우리 늦어도 거기에 일곱 시 전까지는 도착해야해.

③ **according to**

It was smooth sailing. Everything went according to plan.

순탄했지. 모든 게 계획대로 진행이 되었어.

☑ according to some doctors: 몇몇 의사들의 말에 따르면

Day 109

① **all the way**

What happened to this? This window won't close all the way.

이게 왜 이러지? 이 창문이 다(완전히, 끝까지) 안 닫혀.

☑ I lost my wallet and I had to walk all the way home.
나 지갑 잃어버려서 집까지 쭉 걸어왔어.

② **awkward**

I feel awkward when I'm with a stranger.

나는 모르는 사람하고 있으면 어색해.

③ **a piece of**

Could you get me a piece of paper, please?

나 종이 한 장만 갖다 줄래?

☑ a piece of: 한 장, 한 조각

☑ a bottle of / a couple of / a glass of

Day 110

① **around the corner**

Christmas is just around the corner.

곧 크리스마스야.

② **at a time**

Try to do one thing at a time!

한 번에 하나씩만 해!

③ **at once**

I can't do everything at once.

내가 모든 것을 한번에(한꺼번에) 할 수 없어.

☑ Do it at once! 그것을 당장 해!(즉시)

Day 111

① a sense of

It took several days to finish a 2000 piece puzzle but I had this great sense of accomplishment.

2000 피스 퍼즐 끝내는 데 며칠이 걸렸지만 큰 성취감이 있더군.

☑ a sense of+st: ~감

- a sense of responsibility: 책임감
- a sense of guilt: 죄책감

② as well as

My family as well as my friends were all there to see my performance.

우리가족하고 내 친구들 모두 나의 공연을 보기위해 거기에 왔었어.

③ air conditioning(=an air conditioner/AC)

It's usually cool inside as there's air conditioning everywhere.

에어컨이 다 있어서 실내는 보통 시원해.

Day 112

① **annoy**

It's really annoying when one or two mosquitoes buzzing around my head when sleeping.

잠잘 때 한, 두 마리 모기가 내 머리 주위에서 윙윙거리면 진짜 짜증나.

☑ annoy: ~를/을 화나게 만들다

- It annoys me / I'm annoyed

② **all-time**

My all-time favorite movie is E.T. I've seen it four times and I shed tears every time I watched it.

나의 인생 영화는 E.T야. 지금까지 네 번을 봤는데 볼 때마다 울었어.

☑ all time [high/low] 역대 [최고/최하]

- Who's your all time favorite singer?
  네가 가장 좋아하는(지금까지 늘) 좋아하는 가수는 누구니?

③ **after all**

I know you have many friends who would give you good advice when you need some. But after all it's your life. You decide!

너에게 좋은 조언을 해줄 친구들이 많다는 것을 알아. 하지만 결국엔 너의 인생이야. 네가 결정을 해야 돼.

Day 113

① **as simple as**

If you want to be a good English speaker speak in English. It's as simple as that.

영어짱이 되고 싶으면 영어로 말해. 간단해!

② **addictive**

This candy is addictive.

이 사탕이 중독성이 있고만.

☑ be addicted to+[명사/동사ing]

③ **act like**

Why did you act like you knew where it was?

너 왜 그곳이 어디 있는지 아는 것처럼 굴었니?

☑ act like: 처럼 행동하다

Day 114

① **athletic**

I'm not athletic. But I enjoy watching sports games.

난 운동은 잘 못하지만 운동경기를 보는 것은 좋아해.

☑ athletic: 운동을 잘하는

② **Are you saying … ?**

Are you saying that if we don't do anything about climate change now it'll be out of control in nine years?

우리가 지금 기후변화에 대해 아무것도 하지 않으면 9년 후에는 손쓸 수 없는 상황이 될 거라는 거니?

③ **apparently**

Apparently, he knows something that we don't.

모르긴 몰라도 분명히 그는 우리가 모르는 무언가를 아는듯해.

☑ apparently: 확실한 증거는 없지만

Day 115

① all of a sudden

The weather changed all of a sudden. It was a bright sunny day but suddenly It was pouring.

날씨가 갑자기 변했어. 햇볕이 좋은날이었는데 갑자기 굵은 빗줄기가 퍼부었어.

② act up

My computer is acting up again.

내 컴퓨터가 또 말썽이야.

☑ act up: (기계, 몸 등) 고장 나다, 문제가 생기다 / (사람이) 말썽을 부리다

- My allergies acted up when I had some seafood yesterday.
  어제 해산물을 먹었을 때 알레르기가 도졌어.
- He acts up a lot. 그는 말썽을 많이 부려.

③ all year round(=throughout the year)

The place has lots of tourists all year round.

그곳은 일 년 내내 관광객들로 붐벼.

Day 116

① **at the crack of dawn**(=at dawn/early morning)

We left home at the crack of dawn.

우리는 새벽에 집에서 출발했어.

② **at**(=on) **the tip of my tongue**

I know what it is but it's at the tip of my tongue.

나 그게 뭔지 알아 근데 입에서만 맴돌고 생각이 안 나네.

③ **accept**

I apologized him but he didn't accept it.

내가 그에게 사과를 했지만 그는 받아들이지 않았어.

☑ accept: 받아들이다/인정하다/수락하다

Day 117

① add to

Should I add some more sentences to my story?

내 스토리에 문장들을 좀 더 넣어야 할까?

☑ add ~ to: 추가하다/덧붙이다

· I got lost on the way here and to add insult to injury, my battery went dead.
여기에 오는 도중에 길을 잃었고 설상가상으로 휴대폰 배터리도 나갔었어.

② anything but

She eats anything but bread.

그녀는 (다 먹는데) 빵만 안 먹어.

↔ She eats nothing but bread. 그녀는 (다른 건 아무것도 안 먹는데) 빵만 먹어.

☑ She was anything but kind. 그녀는 전혀 친절하지 않았어.

③ at will

I saw an English man on TV who can fart at will.

나 텔레비전에서 방귀를 자유자재로 뀔 수 있는 영국남자를 봤어.

☑ at will: 맘대로, 마음 내키는 대로

Day 118

① **appreciate**

I really appreciate it.

정말 감사하게 생각합니다.

② **at the same time**

It's hard for me to listen to something and write it down at the same time.

나는 뭔가를 들으면서 동시에 그것을 쓰는 게 어려워.

③ **adjust to**

Did you have trouble adjusting to your new school?

너 새 학교에 적응하느라 힘들었니?

☑ adjust to: 적응하다

☑ adjust: 무언가를 더 만족스럽게 조정·조절하다

· adjust [the angle/the chair/the volume …]

Day 119

① apply

My uncle applied to that company.

우리 삼촌이 그 회사에 지원했었어.

☑ apply: 지원하다/적용하다

☑ It doesn't apply to you. 그것은 너한테 적용이 안 돼.

☑ apply to + place

apply for + thing

② agree

Do you agree with him?

그의 말에 동의하니?

☑ agree: ~에 동의하다

☑ agree [with/about/on/to/that/w의문사]

③ air out

You should air out your place at least once or twice a day.

하루에 한두 번은 집을 환기시켜야해.

☑ air out: 환기를 시키다

Day 120

① **be aware of**

You should be aware of what you're doing otherwise you'll easily waste your time.

네가 무엇을 하고 있는지를 잘 알아야 해 그렇지 않으면 너의 시간을 쉽게 낭비하게 돼.

☑ be aware of: 인식하다, 자각하다

② **be tired of**(=be sick and tired of)

I'm tired of eating the same dish for lunch every single day.

난 매일 똑같은 점심을 먹는 것에 질렸어.

☑ be tired of: 싫증난, 질린

③ **be full of**

The place was full of people. It was too crowded.

그곳은 사람들로 가득 차 있었어. 너무 붐볐지.

☑ be filled with: 완전히 차 있는 느낌

be full of: 완전히는 아니지만 많다는 느낌

Day 121

① **by 동사ing**

We can stay healthy by eating properly and moving a lot.

우리는 제대로 먹고 많이 움직임으로써 건강을 유지할 수 있어.

☑ by 동사ing: ~을/를 해서, 함으로써

② **be ready**

I am ready to hear. Go ahead!

나 들을 준비됐어. 어서 말해봐!

☑ be ready for 명사

③ **blow your nose**

Don't sniffle! Blow your nose!

코 훌쩍거리지 말고 코를 풀어!

☑ blow(입으로/자연적으로): 바람이 불다 / 때리다 / 망치다

- Before blow the candles make a wish! 촛불 끄기 전에 소원을 빌어!
- I blew it. 망쳤어.

Day 122

① **be hard on sb**

I think I was too hard on my younger sister.

내가 동생한테 너무 심하게 굴었나봐.

☑ be hard on+sb: ~에게 심하게 대하다

② **by oneself**

When do you think you can travel by yourself?

너는 언제쯤 혼자서 여행할 수 있을 것 같아?

☑ by [myself / herself / himself / themselves / ourselves]

- She sent me pears that she grew herself.
  그녀가 나에게 그녀가 직접 키운 배를 보내줬어.

③ **be proud**

You're in your 20s and you've already saved that amount of money? You must be proud of yourself.

너는 20대인데 벌써 그만큼의 돈을 모았다고? 너 자신이 자랑스럽겠다.

☑ be proud: ~이 자랑스러운

☑ be proud [to 동사원형/that 주어+동사]

Day 123

① break out

The war broke out in 1950.

그 전쟁은 1950년에 일어났어.

☑ break out: 싸움·불·얼굴 종기 등 안 좋은 것이나 일이 갑자기 발생하다(생기다)

- My skin often breaks out in the spring time.
  내 피부는 봄에 자주 트러블이 생겨.

② butter up

Don't butter me up! I won't let you go there.

나한테 아첨하지 마! 너 거기 못가.

☑ butter up: 아첨하다, 아부하다

③ be good at

Are you good at fixing things?

너는 물건 고치는 것을 잘하니?

Day 124

① **be interested in**

I'm interested in music, especially K-pop.

나는 음악에 관심이 있어, 특히 한국 대중가요.

☑ He is into Korean history these days.그는 요즘 한국사에 빠져있어.

② **be famous for**

Korea is famous for 김치, K-pop and many more.

한국은 김치, 케이 팝 그리고 많은 것들로 유명해.

③ **be good for**

Fermented food is good for your health.

발효식품은 건강에 좋아.

Day 125

① be about to

I was about to go out when I got your call.

나 너한테 전화 왔을 때 막나가려던 중이었어.

☑ be about to: 막 ~하려는 참이다

② by the way

By the way, how did your test go?

그런데(그나저나) 너 시험 어떻게 됐어?

③ be always 동사ing

He is always complaining about lunch menu.

그는 항상 점심식사 메뉴에 대해 불평을 해.

☑ be always 동사ing: 특히 안 좋은 습관 등을 자주하다

Day 126

① **by the time**

By the time we got there, it had already started.

우리가 거기에 도착했을 즈음에는 그것은 이미 시작해 있었어.

② **be similar to**

The story is sort of similar to the one I read before.

그 얘기는 내가 전에 읽었던 것과 비슷해.

③ **be different from**(=than/to)

It's okay to be different from other people as long as you have a healthy mindset.

네가 건강한 마음자세만 가지고 있다면 다른 사람들과 달라도 돼.

☑ It's the same as: ~와 같은

Day 127

① **be dying to**

I'm dying to see my presents.

나는 내 선물들을 보고 싶어 죽겠어.

☑ I'm dying for some sweets. 나 단거 먹고 싶어 죽겠어.

② **believe it or not**

Believe it or not, I'm self quarantining at home.

믿기 힘들겠지만, 나 집에서 자가 격리 중이야.

③ **be gone**

My highlighter is gone. Have you seen it?

내 형광펜이 없어졌어. 너 봤니?

☑ be gone: 떠나다, 갔다, 없어지다

Day 128

① bother

I didn't want to bother you!

널 귀찮게 하고 싶지 않았어.

☑ bother: 거슬리다/짜증나다

☑ It really bothers me that my sister sings everytime I read books.
내가 책 읽을 때 마다 동생이 노래를 부르는 게 진짜 짜증나.

② book

Do you think I should book in advance?

너 생각에는 내가 미리 예약을 해야 할 것 같니?

☑ book: 예약하다

☑ book a table

book tickets for+[sb/st]

book the holiday

③ busy 동사ing

He is always busy making something.

그는 항상 뭔가를 만드느라 바빠.

☑ busy 동사ing: ~하느라 바쁜

☑ busy 동사ing / busy with 명사

Day 129

① **be responsible for**

Who do you think is responsible for this?

이것의 책임이 누구한테 있는 것 같아?

= Who's to blame?

☑ be responsible for: ~에 책임이 있는

② **be in one's 20's**

I think she is in her 20's.

내 생각엔 그녀는 20대인 거 같아.

☑ in my 30's / in his 40's / in their 50's

③ **boiling hot**

It's boiling hot in summer.

여름엔 완전 찌는 듯이 더워.

= It's scorching hot. / It's sweltering.

Day 130

① be obsessed with

He is obsessed with grades.

그는 성적에 너무 집착해.

② be known as

추석 is Korean thanksgiving day. It's known as 한가위 as well.

추석은 한국의 추수감사절이야. 추석은 또 한가위라고도 불려.

☑ be known as: ~라는 이름으로 알려진

☑ be known for = be famous for: ~로 유명한

- 부산 is known for 부산오뎅

③ bump into(=run into)

Guess, who I bumped into today?

내가 오늘 우연히 누구를 만났게?

☑ bump into: 무언가에 부딪치다

☑ I bumped into my old friend in the mall.
나 쇼핑몰에서 우연히 옛날 친구를 만났어.

Day 131

① **blame**

You shouldn't blame others when it's your fault.

네가 잘못해 놓고 다른 사람들을 탓하면 안 돼.

☑ blame: 비난하다, 탓하다

☑ blame A for B: ~B에 대하여 A를 탓하다

② **be stuck in**

Sorry, I'm late. I was stuck in traffic.

미안해. 늦었어. 길이 막혀가지고.

☑ be stuck in: ~에 갇혀있는, 오도 가도 못하는

☑ be stuck in [the elevator/a situation …]

③ **be covered in**(=be covered with)

Look at all the cars covered in snow.

눈에 쌓인 차들 좀 봐!

☑ be covered in: ~에 덮인

☑ cover: 덮다, 다루다, 포함하다

Day 132

① **be born in**

He was born in 1397.

그는 1397년에 태어났어.

☑ He was born on December 25. 그는 12월25일에 태어났어.

☑ He was born in Korea. 그는 한국에서 태어났어.

② **being**

You're being so childish today. You're not normally like this. What's got into you?

너 오늘 되게 유치하게 군다. 너 원래는 안 이렇잖아. 왜 그러는 거야?

☑ being [rude/silly/selfish …] : 특히 평상시와는 다르게 행동할 때

③ **blindly**(=mindlessly)

People tend to blindly believe what they hear and read online.

사람들은 인터넷에서 그들이 듣고 읽는 것들을 무턱대고 믿는 경향이 있어.

☑ blindly: 아무 생각 없이

Day 133

① be familiar

He looks very familiar. Oh, he was one of my classmates in school.

저 사람 굉장히 낯익은데. 아 학교 다닐 때 우리 반이었어.

☑ be familiar: 낯익은, 익숙한/잘 아는

☑ be familiar to+sb: ~에 익숙한, 낯익은

be familiar with+st: ~를 잘 아는

② back then

Back then, not many people traveled abroad.

예전에는 해외를 여행하는 사람들이 많지 않았어.

③ beat

I can beat you. Shall we bet ice cream on this.

나 너 이길 수 있어. 우리 이걸로 아이스크림 내기할까?

☑ beat: 상대방, 상대팀, 상대 나라등 그 싸움 속의 상대를 이긴 것을 표현할 때.

win: 게임, 시합, 전쟁 등 그 싸움 자체를 이긴 것을 표현할 때.

· win+sb+over : 반대하는 ~을/를 설득하다

Day 134

① **by then**

I'll be back from my math class by then.

그때쯤이면 내가 수학수업 끝나고 돌아 올 거야.

② **be based on**

It is based on scientific principles.

그것은 과학적인 원리를 기반으로 해.

③ **be impressed by**

I was impressed by what she said.

나는 그녀가 한 말에 감명을 받았어.

☑ impressed [by/with]

Day 135

① **basically**

A: What do I need to do here?

B: Basically, all you have to do is wash the veggies.

A: 내가 여기서 뭘 해야 해?

B: 기본적으로 네가 할 것이라곤 야채를 씻는 것밖에 없어.

② **buckle up**

Buckle up otherwise you'll have to pay a fine.

운전 벨트 매 그렇지 않으면 너 벌금내야 할 거야.

③ **break the ice**

In order to break the ice, We played a game.

어색한 분위기를 깨기 위해서 우리는 게임을 했어.

Day 136

① by hand

Is it made by hand or by a machine?

이것은 손으로 만들어졌나요? 아니면 기계로 만들었나요?

☑ I eat pizza with my hands. 난 손으로 피자 먹어.

② be all ears

A: I'm gonna tell you what happened there.

B: I'm all ears.

A: 내가 거기서 무슨 일이 있었는지 말해줄게.

B: 나 완전히 들을 준비돼있어.

☑ We are all ears. / She was all ears.

③ before you know it

Time flies. you'll graduate before you know it.

시간이 정말 빨리 가. 너는 금방 졸업하게 될 거야.

Day 137

① bundle up

Bundle up! It's freezing out there.

많이 껴입어! 밖에 엄청 추워.

② brag about(=show off = boast about 명사 / that 주어+동사)

He's always bragging about his stuff. He's such a show-off.

그는 항상 자신의 물건을 자랑해. 정말 잘난 척 쟁이야.

☑ brag that 주어+동사

③ be supposed to

Where are you? you are supposed to be here by now.

너 지금 어디야? 지금쯤이면 여기에 와 있어야 하잖아.

☑ be supposed to: 해야 한다/~하기로 되어있다 (의무, 책임이 있다)

You're not supposed to eat here. 너 여기서 먹으면 안 돼.

Day 138

① **be made up of**(=consist of)

This book is made up of two parts.

이 책은 두 파트로 구성이 되어있어.

② **be bound to**

There's bound to be lots of traffic here.

여기는 교통이 혼잡할 수밖에 없어.

☑ be bound to: 틀림없이~하게 되다

③ **by far**

I'm sure we'll win. We're by far the best.

우리가 이길게 틀림없어. 우리가 단연코 최고거든.

Day 139

① blow one's mind

Their performance was out of this world. It blew my mind.

그들의 공연은 완전 최고였어. 정말 홀딱 반했어.

② beside the point

That's beside the point. His argument was why he should do such things while the others don't.

그게 요점이 아니야. 그의 주장은 다른 사람들은 안하는데 왜 그가 그런 일을 해야 하는지야.

③ blessing in disguise

It was definitely a blessing in disguise for him to have that stomachache, otherwise he wouldn't have gone to the doctor finding the malignant tumor.

그 복통은 그에게 정말 전화위복이었어. 그 복통 아니었으면 병원에 갈일도 없었고 악성종양을 발견할 수도 없었겠지.

☑ blessing in disguise: 좋지 않은 일이 좋은 일이 되다

Day 140

① boss around

I don't want to boss people around telling them what to do.

난 사람들에게 이래라 저래라 하며 명령하기 싫어.

② bite the bullet

There are times where we should bite the bullet and do what we don't want to do.

우리는 모두 하고 싶지 않은 일을 꾹 참고 해야 할 때가 있지.

☑ bite the bullet: 어려운 일, 하고 싶지 않은 일을 참고하다

③ Don't beat around the bush(=cut to the chase)

Don't beat around the bush! Just tell me what he said.

빙빙 돌려 말하지 마! 그냥 그가 뭐라고 했는지 말해줘.

Day 141

① bear in mind

Bear in mind that there won't be any place where you can buy Korean food.

한국음식을 파는 곳이 없다는 거 기억해(명심해).

② belong to

A: Do you belong to any club?
B: I'm a member of an art club.

A: 너 동아리 하는 거 있니?
B: 나 미술 동아리 해.

☑ belong to: ~에 속하다

③ back and forth

The teacher always walks back and forth while talking.

그 선생님은 말할 때 항상 왔다갔다 걸어 다녀.

☑ back and forth: 앞, 뒤 혹은 좌, 우로 왔다갔다

Day 142

① behave oneself

You should behave yourself! You're not a baby.

똑바로 행동해! 너는 아기가 아니야.

② believe in

Do you believe in God?

너는 신을 믿니?

☑ believe in: 존재를 믿다/신뢰하다

- I believe what you said. 난 네가 한말을 믿어.

③ be considered [형/명]

It's considered rude(bad manners) to slurp in many countries.

후루룩 소리 내며 먹는 것은 많은 나라들에서 무례하게 여겨져.

☑ be considered: ~로 여겨지다, 생각되다

Day 143

① **clean up**(=clean)

I need to clean up. I'm having my friends over today.

나 청소해야 해. 오늘 친구가 놀러오거든.

☑ clean up: 청소하다(일반적인), 닦다

clean out: 무엇인가의 속, 안에 있는 것을 치우다

clean off: 표면을 닦다

clean away: 더러운 무언가를 닦아내다

② **clear up**

The sky has cleared up. Shall we go out?

하늘이 개었어. 밖에 나갈까?

☑ [weather/skin/illness/problems …] clear up

③ **close**(즈)(=shut)

The store closes at 11.

그 가게는 오후 11시에 문을 닫아.

☑ Many pharmacies are closed on Sundays.
많은 약국들이 일요일에는 영업을 안 해.

☑ The store is close(스) to my place. 그 가게는 우리 집에서 가까워.

Day 144

① come to think of it

Come to think of it, It's(has) been a while since I saw Chris.
Have you heard from him recently?

생각해보니까, 크리스를 본지 꽤 됐어. 너 최근에 그에게 소식 들은 거 있니?

② count sb in

A: Who wants to play dodge ball?
B: Count me in!

A: 피구할 사람?
B: 나 끼워줘!

↔ Count [me/her/him/them/us] out. 나는 빼줘.

③ coincidence

A: Your name is Kate? My name is Kate too.
B: What a coincidence!

A: 너의 이름이 캐잇이라고? 내 이름도 케잇이야.
B: 정말 우연이네!

☑ It's a coincidence ….

Day 145

① **confused**

I'm a bit confused. Which one is Skeleton, the one that lying on the back or lying face down?

나 좀 헷갈려. 어느 게 스켈레톤이야 하늘보고 눕는 거 아니면 엎드리는 거?

☑ It's confusing

② **complicated**

The instructions are so complicated. I don't understand them at all.

그 설명서가 너무 복잡해. 난 전혀 이해를 못하겠어.

☑ complicated: 이해하기가 힘든, 어려운

complex: 구조가 복잡한, 단순하지 않은

③ **could use**

I could use a glass of water. I'm really thirsty.

물 한잔만 마셨으면 좋겠다. 목이 너무 말라.

☑ could use: 원하다, 필요하다

Day 146

① collapse

The small bridge collapsed because of the heavy rain.

그 작은 다리가 폭우에 무너졌어.

☑ collapse: 물리적/추상적인 것이 무너지다

② come over

My cousin is coming over this weekend. I'm so excited.

내 사촌이 이번 주말에 와. 너무 신나.

☑ come over (to+sb's place): 누가 집에 오다

☑ I'm having my friends over today. 오늘 내 친구들이 와.

③ call sb back

I'll call you back later. I'm in the middle of something.

내가 다시 전화해줄게. 지금 뭐하고 있는 중이거든.

Day 147

① can't afford to

We can't afford to just sit and talk about climate change. We should take action to save our ailing earth.

우리가 그냥 앉아서 기후변화에 대해 얘기하고 있을 여유가 없어. 우리의 병들어 있는 지구를 살리기 위해서 뭔가 조치를 취해야해.

☑ can't afford to: ~할 여유가 없다

② chances are

Chances are they won't show up there on time.

그들이 거기에 제시간에 나타나지 않을 확률이 높아.

☑ chances are: 가능성이 높은

③ catch up on

I met her for the first time in a long time. It was nice catching up on each other's lives over lunch.

그녀를 오래간만에 만났거든. 점심 먹으면서 서로 그동안에 밀렸던 얘기를 할 수 있어서 너무 좋았어.

☑ catch up on: 하지 못했던, 밀려있던 것을 하다

catch up on some house chores: 밀린 집안일을 하다

catch up on sleep: 밀린 잠을 자다

Day 148

① can't go wrong

You can't go wrong with a bowl of cold noodles in the summer time.

여름에 냉면 한 그릇은 항상 옳아.

☑ can't go wrong with+명사

can't go wrong 동사ing

② cut corners

Try not to cut corners whatever you do. Do your utmost to make your work outstanding.

네가 무엇을 하든 지름길을 선택하지 마. 너의 최고의 결과물을 만들기 위해 최선을 다해봐.

③ can relate to

A: I felt terribly homesick in the beginning of the time there.

B: I can totally relate to that.

A: 거기에 있던 처음 얼마동안은 심한 향수병을 겪었어.

B: 나 완전히 이해해./나도 그랬어.

☑ can relate to: ~에 공감하다

Day 149

① **cost**

It cost much more than I was expecting.

내 예상보다 돈이 훨씬 더 많이 들었어.

☑ cost/cost/cost: 돈이 들다, 필요하다, 잃다 / 비용, 희생

② **certain**

There are certain words that are hard to pronounce.

발음하기 힘든 어떤 특정한 단어들이 있어.

☑ certain: 확실한, 어떤 특정한

☑ a certain: 어느정도

· A certain amount of carbs are necessary for your health.
어느정도의 탄수화물은 너의 건강을 위해서 필요해.

③ **call it a day**

Let's call it a day!

오늘은 그것으로 마무리하자!

☑ = Let's wrap it up!

Day 150

① **can't take one's eyes off**

I couldn't take my eyes off it. It was the best view ever.

나는 그것에서 눈을 뗄 수가 없었어. 그것은 역대 최고의 경치였어.

② **carry on**(=continue/keep~ ing)

If you carry on eating like that, you'll end up not only getting fat but also getting sick.

만약에 네가 계속 그렇게 먹으면 살이 찌는 것뿐만이 아니라 병도 걸리게 될 거야.

☑ carry on: 계속~하다

☑ a carry-on 기내에 가지고 들어갈 수 있는 가방

③ **can't help**

I know I shouldn't eat lots of chocolate but I can't help it.

내가 초콜릿을 많이 먹으면 안 되는 것을 알지만 어쩔 수가 없어.

Day 151

① contrary to

Contrary to what we believe, watching TV can be good, especially something fun and funny.

우리가 생각하는 것과는 반대로 텔레비전을 보는 것이 좋을 수 있어, 특히 재밌거나 웃긴 것들.

② come down with

I think I'm coming down with a cold.

나 감기 걸린 것 같아.

☑ come down with: 병에 걸리다(막 시작하려할 때)

come down with something

③ cut down on

I think you should cut down on those supplements.

나는 네가 영양보충제 섭취를 줄여야 한다고 생각해.

☑ cut down on: ~을/를 줄이다

cut down on [smoking/spending/sugar …].

Day 152

① compare to

A: 칠득 is taller than me. I'm so jealous.

B: Don't compare yourself to others! You're good enough.

A: 칠득이가 나보다 키가 더 커. 너무 부러워.

B: 다른 사람들하고 너를 비교하지 마! 너는 충분히 훌륭해.

☑ compare to: ~와 비교하다

- Compared to the previous movie, I think this one is not bad.
  지난번 영화와 비교하면 이번 건 나쁘지 않은 것 같아.

② can't wait

I can't wait to go there.

거기에 빨리 가고 싶다.

☑ I can't wait for my birthday. 빨리 내 생일이 왔으면 좋겠다.

③ come up with

Try to come up with some stories in English when you're in bed trying to sleep or on a bus or the subway.

네가 자려고 누워있을 때 혹은 버스나 지하철에서 영어로 이야기를 생각해내려고 노력해봐.

☑ come up with: 아이디어, 계획 등을 생각해내다/돈을 마련하다

Day 153

① a catch

There's always a catch when something is too good to be true.

뭔가 너무 좋을 때는 함정(꿍꿍이)같은 게 늘 있게 마련이야.

☑ What's the catch? 무슨 꿍꿍이야? (숨겨진 의도가 뭐야)

② calm down

Calm down! I haven't finished yet.

진정해! 내 말 아직 안 끝났어.

☑ calm+sb+down ~를 진정시키다

③ care about

Of course, I care about my cats but I can't care for them 24/7.

물론 내 고양이들이 소중하지만 내가 고양이들을 항상 돌봐줄 수는 없어.

☑ care about: 걱정하다/신경 쓰다
care for: 보살피다

Day 154

① **come to one's senses**

When will you come to your senses?

너 정신 언제 차릴래?

☑ come to one's senses: 정신 차리다

- I wish you would come to your senses. 난 네가 정신을 차렸으면 좋겠다.

② **can't stand**

Summer is my least favorite season because I can't stand the heat.

여름은 내가 가장 좋아하지 않는 계절이야 왜냐하면 나는 더위를 잘 못 견뎌.

☑ can't stand: 참을 수가 없다

③ **cut in line**

Don't cut in line! We should wait in line.

새치기하지 마! 우리 줄서서 기다려야해.

☑ cut in line: 새치기하다

Day 155

① can't put one's finger on

I can't put my finger on it but he is kind of shady.

딱 꼬집어 말할 수는 없지만 그는 어딘가 미심쩍은 데가 있어.

② cancel out

His brag cancels out his good deed.

그의 자랑은 그가 한 좋은 일의 공을 다 무너뜨려(상쇄해).

③ cater to

This book caters to people who want to see the big picture of English.

이 책은 영어의 큰 그림을 보고 싶은 사람들에게 맞추어진 책이야.

☑ cater to: ~에 맞추다

Day 156

① **cut sb some slack**(=give sb a break/take it easy on sb)

Please cut me some slack if I mess up. I've never made 떡볶이 before.

망쳐도 나 좀 봐줘. 나 떡볶이 한 번도 안 만들어봤어.

☑ let it slide: 사정을 봐주다, 여유를 주다

② **count**

It's not how much you learn but how much you remember that counts.

얼마만큼 배우느냐가 아니라 얼마만큼 네가 기억하느냐가 더 중요해.

☑ count: 가치가 있다, 중요하다, 숫자를 세다

③ **chip in**

We chipped in to get some presents for parents' day.

어버이날 선물을 사기위해 우리는 같이 돈을 냈어.

Day 157

① **Cut it out!**

Cut it out! I've got to finish this.

그만해! 나 이거 끝내야해.

② **count on**(=rely on)

Even though she is younger than me, I can count on her.

그녀가 나보다 어리지만 난 그녀를 믿고 의지해.

③ **check in**

We're going to check in at 11 a.m on Saturday and check out at 10 a.m the next day.

우리는 토요일 오전 11시에 체크인해서 그 다음날 오전 10시에 체크아웃할거야.

☑ check in: 숙박수속을 밟다 / check out: 숙박시설에서 계산하고 나오다

☑ check in: 짧게 대화하다

check out: 도서관에서 책을 대출하다/살펴보다

check on: 무언가 혹은 사람이 괜찮은지 확인하다

Day 158

① **cheer up**

That music always cheers me up whenever I feel down.

내가 기분이 울적할 때면 저 음악이 항상 나를 다시 기분 좋게 해.

② **complain about**

There's no point in complaining about the weather.

날씨에 대해 불평해봤자 소용없어.

☑ complain about: 불평하다

③ **concentrate on**

It was hard to concentrate on my studies with all that noise.

그 소음 때문에 공부에 집중하기가 힘들었어.

☑ concentrate on: 에 집중하다

Day 159

① **do the dishes**(=wash the dishes)

My least favorite chore is to do the dishes.

내가 가장 싫어하는 일이 설거지하는 거야.

☑ do the dishes: 설거지하다

② **do the laundry**

Who is in charge of doing the laundry?

누가 빨래 담당이야?

☑ do the laundry: 빨래하다

③ **depend on**

A: Mom, please say yes!
B: It depends on what you're going to say.

A: 엄마, 'Yes'라고 말해줘!
B: 네가 뭐라고 하느냐에 달렸지.

☑ It depends on the situation. 상황에 따라 달라.
It depends on one's mood. 기분에 따라 달라.

Day 160

① decide

Have you decided what to buy for your parents?

부모님에게 무엇을 사드릴지 정했니?

☑ decide+[to+동사원형/that 주어+동사/w의문사]

② Don't get me wrong

Don't get me wrong! I didn't look at your cell phone.

오해하지 마! 나 너 휴대폰 안 봤어.

☑ get sb/st wrong: 오해하다 (=misunderstand)

③ do sightseeing(=go sightseeing)

We ate lots of seafood and did some sightseeing.

우리는 해산물도 많이 먹고 관광도 했어.

Day 161

① divide into

We were divided into two teams, blue and white. I was on the blue team.

우리는 청팀과 백팀 두 팀으로 나뉘었는데. 난 청팀이었어.

② doze off

I must have dozed off.

나 깜빡 잤나봐.

☑ doze off: 깜빡 잠이 들다

③ Did you know

Did you know that ramen is the most popular snack among middle and high school boys?

중고등학교 남학생들 사이에서 가장 인기 있는 간식이 라면이라는 거 너 알고 있었니?

Day 162

① disgust

A: I put five slices of cheese on top of my 라면

B: What? Ew, that's disgusting.

A: 난 라면위에 치즈 다섯 장 올려서 먹어.

B: 뭐? 윽, 구역질 나려 그래.

☑ disgust: 역겨움/역겹게 하다

② don't feel good(=be/feel under the weather)

I don't feel so good(well) today. I might have to take medicine.

오늘 몸 상태가 안 좋아. 약을 먹어야 할까봐.

☑ 기분이 안 좋은: I'm not in a good mood.

③ don't quote me on that

A: What's the 50th state of the US?

B: I think Hawaii. But don't quote me on that.

A: 미국의 50번째 주가 뭐지?

B: 하와이인 것 같은데. 나도 확실하진 않아(다른 곳에 가서 말하진 말아라).

Day 163

① **drip**

I turned the tap off but it's still dripping.

내가 수도꼭지를 잠갔는데도 물이 똑똑 흘러.

② **do the hard way**

Why are you always doing things the hard way? Call a technician!

너는 왜 그렇게 일을 항상 어렵게 하냐? 그냥 기술자를 불러!

③ **don't get your hopes up**

I'm going to make some cookies but don't get your hopes up!

내가 쿠키 만들 건데 기대는 하지 마!

Day 164

① dwell on

You don't have time to dwell on what other people have said to you. Focus on your goals, your dreams!

다른 사람들이 너에게 한 말에 연연해할 시간이 없어. 너의 목표 너의 꿈에 집중해!

☑ dwell on the past: 과거에 연연하다

② deserve

You deserve it. You've been working so hard. It's time to have fun.

넌 자격이 있어! 너 지금까지 열심히 일했잖아(공부). 이제 즐겨.

☑ He deserves the punishment. 그는 벌을 받을 만해.

③ down in the dumps

I felt down in the dumps for the last few days but I feel better now.

지난 며칠 동안 기분이 울적했는데 지금은 좋아졌어.

☑ down in the dumps: 기분이 울적한, 우울한

Day 165

① **dip**

Which do you prefer, dipping it in the sauce or pouring the sauce over it?

너는 소스에 찍어먹는 것을 더 좋아하니 아니면 소스를 부어먹는 것을 더 좋아하니?

☑ dip: 담그다

② **drop sb off**

Could you drop me off here?

저 여기서 내려주세요!

③ **duck**

A ball! Duck!

공이다! 피해!

☑ duck: 머리를 숙여 뭔가를 피하다

Day 166

① **do one's best**(=commit to ing/commit oneself)

I'll do my best to improve my English skills during this summer vacation.

나는 이번 여름방학동안 나의 영어실력을 향상시키기 위해 최선을 다 할 거야.

② **drop out**

He dropped out of college but became a successful businessman.

그는 대학을 중퇴했지만 성공한 사업가가 되었어.

☑ drop out of the [race/school …]: ~을/를 하다가 중도에 그만두다

③ **dress up**

I've dressed up for the wedding.

그 결혼식을 위해서 차려입었어.

☑ I dressed up as a ghost. 귀신 복장을 하다.

Day 167

① **due to**

People's unhappiness is due to greed.

사람들의 불행은 욕심 때문이야.

☑ This homework is due on Monday. 이 숙제 월요일까지 해야 해.

② **die down**

I think we should wait until the rain dies down. If we go out now, we'll get soaked.

비가 잦아들 때까지 기다려야할 것 같아. 지금 나가면 흠뻑 젖겠어.

☑ die down: 강도, 정도가 약해지다, 잦아들다

☑ die out: 멸종되다

die off: 점점 수가 감소하다가 멸종되다

③ **deal with**

This book tells you how to deal with difficult situations.

이 책은 어려운 상황들을 대처하는 방법에 대해서 말하고 있어.

☑ deal with: 처리하다, 다루다, 상대하다

Day 168

① effort

There is no free lunch. It means everything takes effort.

공짜는 없어. 그것은 모든 일에는 노력이 필요하다는 뜻이야.

☑ make an effort / put effort: 노력을 하다

② even

He wears that hat all the time, even at home.

그는 그 모자를 항상 써 심지어 집에서도

③ enjoy

Do you enjoy cooking or eating?

너는 요리하는 것을 즐기니 아니면 먹는 것을 즐기니?

☑ enjoy+[명사/동사ing]

Day 169

① **every other day**(=every two days)

I go hiking every other day.

나는 이틀에 한 번씩 하이킹을 가.

☑ · The bus runs every five minutes. 저 버스는 5분마다 와.

· The Olympic Games and the World Cup take place every four years. 올림픽하고 월드컵은 4년마다 열려.

② **eat out**(=go out to eat)

My mom is a great cook so we rarely eat out.

우리 엄마가 요리를 정말 잘하기 때문에 우리는 외식을 거의 안 해.

☑ eat out: 외식하다

③ **exactly**

That's exactly what I mean.

그게 바로 내말이야.

☑ exactly: 정확하게

Day 170

① enough

My sister wasn't tall enough to go on that ride.

내 동생은 그 놀이기구를 타기에 키가 충분히 크지 않았아.

☑ enough: 충분한

Do we have enough plates? 우리 접시가 충분히 있나?

☑ 형용사/부사 + enough » 예) smart enough / fast enough

enough + 명사 » 예) enough water

② explain

Could you explain it one more time, please?

그거 한번만 더 설명해주시겠어요?

☑ explain: 설명하다

explain+st+to+sb / explain+w의문사

③ embarrass

I was so embarrassed to dance in front of many people.

많은 사람들 앞에서 춤추는 게 정말 창피했어.

☑ embarrass: 창피한/민망한

- I'm embarrassed. 민망해.
- It's embarrassing ~ . ~가 민망해.

Day 171

① either

A: I don't like baseball.

B: I don't like it either.

A: 나 야구 싫어해.

B: 나도 싫어해(=Me neither).

☑ either: 부정문에서 '나도' 또는 '둘 중 하나', '둘 다'

- We can either go to the park or go to the library.
  우리는 공원에 가거나 도서관에 갈 수 있어.

② expired

A: It's expired.

B: I know but it hasn't gone bad.

A: 이거 날짜 지났어.

B: 알아 근데 그거 안 상했어.

③ easier said than done

A: Try to be original. You know "Think outside the box".

B: That's easier said than done.

A: 독창적이려고 노력해봐. 알잖아, 새로운 사고를 하라!

B: 말이 쉽지.

Day 172

① **end up**

Try not to skip any meal, you'll end up overeating for the next meal.

식사를 거르지 않도록 해, 다음 식사 때 과식하게 돼.

☑ end up: 의 결과로 ~하게 되다

② **every now and then**

Every now and then, we all need carefree times where we can be totally free from work and all the worries to recharge.

가끔 재충전을 위해서 우리는 일과 모든 걱정들에서 완전히 자유로울 수 있는 시간이 필요해.

③ **everyone but+sb**

Everyone but you knows about this exercise.

너만 빼고 이 운동 다 알아.

Day 173

① eyeball

A: How much flour do we need?

B: I don't use a recipe. I just eyeball it.

A: 우리 밀가루가 얼마큼 필요하지?

B: 나는 기준(요리법)은 없어. 그냥 눈대중으로 해.

☑ eyeball: 눈대중으로 하다

② empty out

Can you empty out the box? I need to use it.

그 박스 좀 비어줄래? 나 그거 써야 돼.

☑ empty out: 속에 있는 것을 비우다

③ especially

I like all fruit especially summer fruit.

나는 과일은 다 좋아해 특히 여름과일.

Day 174

① early bird

Are you an early bird or a night owl?

너는 아침형 인간이니 아니면 올빼미형(밤에 활동이 많은)이니?

② eventually

You don't need to take any medicine when you get a cold. It'll eventually heal itself.

감기에 걸렸을 때 약을 안 먹어도 돼. 그것은 결국엔 저절로 나아.

☑ eventually: 결국에, 드디어

③ expand one's horizons

Meeting new people and visiting new places are good ways to expand your horizons.

새로운 사람들을 만나고 새로운 곳을 가는 것은 너의 시야를 넓히는 좋은 방법이야.

☑ expand one's horizons: 시야를 넓히다

Day 175

① **follow suit**

Don't just follow suit! Find your own interest and talent.

남들을 그냥 따라하지 마! 너 자신의 흥미와 재능을 찾아.

☑ follow suit: 남이 하는 대로 따라하다

② **for example**(=for instance)

There are some ways to save water. For example, you can use a cup when you brush your teeth.

물을 아낄 수 있는 방법들이 있어. 예를 들면 이를 닦을 때 컵을 쓰는 거야.

③ **forget**

I forgot what my homework is.

나 내 숙제가 뭔지 잊어버렸어.

☑ forget+동사ing: 이미 한 것을 잊다
forget to: ~할 것을 잊다

Day 176

① from now on

From now on, I'm not going to use any bad language.

나 이제부터 그 어떤 욕도 안 할 거야.

☑ from now on: 지금부터 계속 ~

② feel like

I don't feel like going out today.

나 오늘 밖에 안 나가고 싶어.

☑ feel like+동사ing: 하고 싶은 기분이 들다

③ find out

I found out who ate my 떡볶이.

내 떡볶이를 누가 먹었는지 알아냈어.

☑ find out: (우연히) 알아내다

- I found my sock under my bed. 내 침대 밑에서 양말 한 짝 찾았어.

Day 177

① **force sb to**

Do your parents force you to learn something that you don't want to?

너의 부모님은 네가 원하지 않는 것을 억지로 배우게 하시니?

☑ force sb to: 억지로 ~하게하다

② **figure out**

There are many ways to learn English but you should figure out the way that suits you the most.

영어 공부하는 방법은 여러 가지가 있지만 너한테 가장 잘 맞는 방법을 네가 알아내야해.

☑ figure out: 알아내다(연구, 생각, 노력 끝에)

③ **for the time being**

I'm going to stop playing video games for the time being.

당분간은 비디오게임을 안 할 거야.

Day 178

① **for some reason**

For some reason, I don't feel like eating sweets.

왜 그런지는 몰라도, 나 단 게 안 먹고 싶어.

② **fall for**

Did you really fall for it? It was obvious that he was lying.

너 진짜 그것에 속았어? 걔가 거짓말하는 게 뻔했는데.

☑ fall for: ~에 속다

③ **frustrated**

I got really frustrated when I couldn't convey my real thoughts when talking to Michael in English.

마이클하고 영어로 얘기할 때 나의 진짜 생각들을 전달할 수 없어서 정말 답답했어.

☑ I am frustrated. 답답해. 짜증나

It's frustrating ~ . ~가 답답해. 짜증나.

Day 179

① **find it**

I find it easy to learn Japanese compared to other languages.

다른 언어들과 비교하면 일본어는 배우기가 쉽더라고.

☑ find it [hard/interesting/fun …]: ~라고 느끼다

② **from time to time**

It's not good to dwell on the past all the time. However, reflecting on what you did and how you did certain things from time to time is necessary.

항상 과거에 연연하는 것은 좋지 않아. 하지만 가끔은 네가 무엇을 했고 어떤 일을 어떻게 했는지에 대해서 돌아보는 것은 필요해.

③ **from the bottom of my heart**

I congratulated him from the bottom of my heart.

난 그를 진심으로 축하해줬어.

Day 180

① for sure

A : Do you think our team will make it to the semi-finals?

B: For sure.

A: 우리 팀이 4강에 진출할 것 같니?

B: 물론이지.

② fall out

My nephew's tooth fell out while he was eating candy.

우리 조카가 사탕 먹다가 이가 하나 빠졌어.

☑ fall out: 이·머리카락 등이 빠지다 / 떨어져 나가다 / 싸우다

☑ fall down: 넘어지다

fall over: ~에걸려 넘어지다

fall off: ~에서 떨어지다

fall for: ~에 속다

③ face the music

It was my fault. I guess I should face the music.

내 잘못이었어. 내가 (나쁜 결과를)감당해야지.

☑ face the music: 자신이 잘못한 일에 대한 결과에 대해 감당하다

Day 181

① far from(=far cry from)

A: Was it a relaxing day?

B: No, far from it.

A: 느긋한 하루였니?

B: 아니, 전혀.

☑ far from: ~와/과는 거리가 먼

② for one's sake

칠득, listen! I'm saying this for your sake.

칠득아, 들어봐! 나는 지금 너를 위해서 말하고 있는 거야.

☑ When you do something, do it for your own sake not for other's sake.
네가 무언가를 할 때 너 자신을 위해서 해, 다른 사람을 위해서 하지 말고.

③ fit it

It didn't take a long time for me to fit in with my new classmates.

새로운 반 친구들과 친해지는데 오래 걸리지 않았어.

☑ fit in: 어울리다/잘 지내다

☑ The couch doesn't fit in with the livingroom.
그 소파는 거실과 어울리지 않아.

Day 182

① fill in

Do I need to fill in all the blanks in this form?

이 양식에 있는 모든 빈칸을 다 써야하나요?

☑ fill in: 작성하다/채우다/대신하다.

② feel free to

Please feel free to ask any questions!

어떤 질문이든 편하게 물어보세요!

☑ feel free to: 자유롭게, 부담 없이~하다

③ from scratch

Try this! I made this cake from scratch.

먹어봐! 이 케잌 내가 처음부터 다 만들었어.

☑ from scratch: 미리 준비된 것 없이 완전히 처음부터

Day 183

① **focus on**

Focus on your goals and dreams!

너의 목표와 꿈에 집중해!

☑ focus: 관심사중에서 하나에 중점을 두다

concentrate: 하고 있는 것에 정신을 집중하다

② **face to face**

Have you talked with him face to face?

그와 만나서 얘기를 해봤니?

☑ face to face: 얼굴을 맞대고, 대면해서

③ **fall asleep**(=doze off)

I fell asleep while reading a book.

책을 읽다가 잠이 들었어.

☑ fall fast asleep 깊이 잠이 들다

Day 184

① **freak out**

I totally freaked out not knowing where to go.

나는 어디로 가야할지 몰라서 완전 당황했어.

☑ freak out: 기겁하다, 놀라다

② **fasten**

Fasten your seatbelt!

안전 벨트 꽉 매!

☑ Fasten your [jacket/belt …].

③ **flock to**

Did you see the news about People flocking into the store to get the new designer bags?

너 새 디자이너 백을 사려고 점포로 몰려드는 사람들에 관한 뉴스 봤니?

☑ flock to: 몰려들다

Day 185

① **from the comfort of your home**

Isn't it wonderful I can get anything from the comfort of my home?

편하게 집에서 모든 것을 살 수 있다는 게 정말 좋지 않니?

② **fall apart**

I bought these shoes a couple of months ago but they've already fallen apart.

나 이 신발 몇 달 전에 샀는데 벌써 해어졌어.

☑ fall apart: 물건, 사업, 관계 등이 안 좋아지다/못쓰게 되다

③ **fingers crossed**

A: I'm going camping this weekend. I hope the weather will be nice.

B: Fingers crossed!

A: 나 이번 주에 캠핑 가. 날씨가 좋았으면 좋겠어.

B: 그러길 바라.(행운을 빌어)

☑ He crossed his fingers. 그는 행운을 빌었다.

Day 186

① **go against**(=be against/oppose/be opposed to)

Some people went against the new policy.

어떤 사람들은 새 정책에 반대했어.

② **go over**

Let's go over the page one more time!

우리 다시 한 번 그 페이지를 자세히 훑어보자!

③ **get one's haircut**

A: Did you get your haircut?

B: Yes, I got a haircut.

A: 너 머리 잘랐니?

B: 응, 나 머리 잘랐어.

☑ I got my computer fixed. 나 컴퓨터 (사람 불러서) 고쳤어.

Day 187

① go 동사ing

I want to go camping but my dad wants to go fishing.

나는 캠핑하러가고 싶은데 우리아빠는 낚시하러가고 싶어 해.

☑ go+동사ing: ~하러가다

② get rid of

What do you do to get rid of stress?

너는 스트레스를 없애기 위해 뭘 하니?

☑ get rid of [old clothes/bad friends …]: 제거하다/없애다

③ get/be used to

He'll get used to this cold weather in no time.

그는 이 추운 날씨에 곧 익숙해질 거야.

☑ get(be) used to+동사ing: ~에 익숙해지다

Day 188

① **get sb st**

Could you get me toilet paper, please?

나 화장실 휴지 좀 갖다 줄래?

② **get around**

I love 서울. Thanks to excellent public transport, it's so easy to get around.

난 서울이 좋아. 아주 잘 되어있는 대중교통덕분에 돌아다니기가 정말 쉽거든.

☑ get around: 돌아다니다

③ **guarantee**

I guarantee that you'll love that place. They have your favorite Korean dish 청국장 and many more.

내가 장담하는데 너 거기 정말 마음에 들어 할 거야. 그곳은 네가 제일 좋아하는 한국음식인 청국장 그리고 다른 많은 것들을 팔아.

Day 189

① **go on a trip**(=travel)

My family and I went on a trip to 부산.

나 가족하고 부산에 여행 갔었어.

☑ go on a trip: 여행을 가다(=take a trip)

go on [a holiday/vacation …]: 휴가가다

☑ go on a roller coaster

② **go+동사원형**

Look! There's your favorite singer over there. Go ask him for an autograph!

봐! 네가 제일 좋아하는 가수 저기 있다. 가서 사인해 달라고 해!

☑ go+동사원형: 가서 ~하다

go see a movie / go brush your teeth

③ **goof around**

It's okay to relax and goof around once in a while.

가끔은 편하게 쉬면서 빈둥거리는 것도 괜찮아.

☑ goof around: 빈둥거리다, 쓸데없는 일이나 장난을 하며 시간을 보내다

Day 190

① **get+비교급**

It's getting cooler.

점점 더 시원해지고 있어.

☑ get [taller/easier/more interesting …]

② **get sb to**

I didn't want to but mom got me to walk my dog Happy.

난 하기 싫었는데 우리 엄마가 우리 개 해피를 산책시키라고 하셨지.

☑ get+sb+to: 누구를 설득하거나 조정해서 ~하게 하다

☑ have+sb+동사원형: ~하게 하다/시키다 (그냥 ask의 개념)

make+sb+동사원형: 누군가를 억지로 ~하게 하다

③ **get along with**

Do you get along with your sister?

너는 여동생과 사이가 좋니?

Day 191

① **get to**

The children will get to see how to grow certain vegetables there and they'll also get to have firsthand experience.

아이들은 거기에서 채소들을 어떻게 키우는지를 보게 될 거야. 또한 그들은 직접 경험을 하게 될 거고.

☑ It was nice to get to know you a bit. 너를 알게 되어서 좋았어.

☑ get to (do st): ~을(를) 할 기회가 주어지다, ~을(를) 할 수 있게 되다

② **get over**

I had a cold but got over it.

나는 감기에 걸렸었는데 다 나았어.

☑ get over [something/someone]
: 병의 상태가 좋아지다 / (나쁜 상황 등에서) 기분이 나아지다

③ **get dressed**

After breakfast, I brush my teeth and get dressed.

아침식사 후에 이를 닦고 옷을 입어.

Day 192

① give away

They're giving away free samples of dumplings.

저기 만두 시식한다.

☑ give away: 무료로 주다

② get together

My family and relatives get together on 추석 and 설날.

우리가족과 친척들은 추석과 설날에 모여.

☑ get together: 모이다

a family get-together: 가족모임

③ get married

The bear became a woman and got married to 환웅.

그 곰은 여자가 되었고 환웅과 결혼을 했어.

☑ get married : 결혼을 하다

☑ get married to ~와 결혼하다

get married with two children 결혼해서 아이가 둘이 있다

- She married him. 그녀는 그와 결혼했어.
- She is married. 그녀는 유부녀야.

Day 193

① go through

When studying English you're bound to go through a time where you feel like you're stuck in the same place without making any progress.

영어를 배울 때 너는 아무런 진척 없이 똑같은 곳에 머물러 있는 듯한 시기를 거치게 될 거야.

☑ go through: 경험하다, 통과하다

☑ go through customs: 세관을 통과하다

② go/fly out the window(=go down the drain/toilet)

If you don't use the words and expressions that you've learned they'll just go out the window.

네가 배운 단어와 표현들을 쓰지 않으면 그것들은 무용지물이 될 거야.

☑ [go/fly] out the window: 없어지다, 사라지다

③ grow on+sb

Vegemite is not for everyone. But with time, it'll definitely grow on you.

베지마이트는 호불호가 있는 음식이야. 하지만 너는 시간이 지나면서 분명히 그것을 좋아하게 될 거야.

☑ grow on+sb: 처음에는 싫었는데 점점 좋아지다

Day 194

① get by

A: I didn't know you speak French.

B: No, I don't. I was able to get by with several words I knew and body language.

A: 네가 프랑스어를 할 수 있는지 몰랐어.

B: 나 못해. 내가 알고 있던 단어 몇 개랑 몸짓으로 그럭저럭 생활할 수 있었어.

☑ get by: 그럭저럭 버티다

② get in the way

Even though 칠득 loves playing video games, he makes sure it doesn't get in the way of his studies.

칠득이는 게임하는 것을 정말 좋아하지만 그것이 공부에 방해가 되지 않도록 철저히 노력해.

☑ get in the way: ~에 방해가 되다

③ get a tan

I put lots of sunscreen before going out but still I got a tan.

외출하기 전에 선크림 많이 발랐는데 그래도 피부가 까맣게 탔어.

Day 195

① **go through the motions**

Every day is your precious gift and class. Don't just go through the motions!

매일이 너의 귀중한 선물이자 수업이야. 그냥 열의 없이 대충 보내지마!

☑ go through the motions: 설렁설렁, 대충하다

② **give off**

It gives off a beautiful smell of phytoncide.

그건 정말 좋은 피톤치드 향이나.

= It has a smell of …

☑ give off: 냄새, 빛, 열, 소리 등을 내다

☑ phytoncide: 파이톤사이ㄷ

③ **go viral**

The video of the singer quickly went viral.

그 가수의 영상이 순식간에 난리가 났어.

☑ go viral: 온라인상에서 빠르게 퍼지다

Day 196

① get off

A: We should get off here.

B: No, next stop.

A: 우리 여기서 내려야 해.

B: 아니야, 다음 정류장이야.

↔ get on the bus (get in a car)

② give it a try(=give it a shot)

Give it a try! I'm sure, you'll love it.

한번 해봐! 너는 틀림없이 좋아할 거야.

③ go ahead

A: Can I use the bathroom?

B: Go ahead!

A: 화장실 좀 써도 될까?

B: 응, 써!

☑ go ahead: 어서 해(먹어, 사용해, 먼저 해.)

Day 197

① **go by**

Time goes by so quickly.

시간은 정말 빨리 가.

☑ go by: 지나가다(시간/공간)

as time goes by / The car went by

② **get emotional**

Everytime I see that scene, I get emotional.

나는 그 장면을 볼 때마다 울컥해.

③ **give sb a hand**(=lend me a hand)

Could you give me a hand? This table is heavier than I thought.

나 좀 도와줄래? 이 탁자가 생각보다 더 무겁네.

Day 198

① go for it

You want to go backpacking, then go for it!

네가 배낭여행을 가고 싶으면 그렇게 해.

☑ go for it: 해봐!

② grow up

I grew up in a city but I often went camping in the countryside.

나는 도시에서 자랐지만 시골로 캠핑을 자주 갔었어.

☑ grow up = be brought up / be raised: 자라다/성장하다

- I didn't have any celebrities that I liked growing up.
  나는 자랄 때 좋아하는 스타가 전혀 없었어.

③ gross

A: I can eat this uncooked.

B: That's gross.

A: 나 이거 안 익히고 그냥 먹을 수 있어.

B: 윽~ 역겨워.

☑ gross: 더러운, 징그러운, 아주 싫은

Day 199

① **grateful**

I'm grateful for what I have and what I don't have.

나는 내가 가진 것과 내가 가지지 않은 것에 대해 감사해.

☑ grateful to / grateful that

② **grab a bite**

Let's grab a bite (to eat) before the movie!

영화보기 전에 뭐 좀 먹자!

☑ grab [a sandwich / a cup of coffee / some sleep …]

③ **go hand in hand**

Wealth and happiness don't necessarily go hand in hand.

부와 행복은 꼭 같이 가는 것은 아니야.

☑ go hand in hand: 관련되다, 함께 가다

Day 200

① **go well with**

A: What goes well with 라면?

B: 찬밥 hands down … or 김치?

A: 라면하고 궁합이 맞는 게 뭘까?

B: 당연히 찬밥이지, 김치인가??

☑ go well with: 색깔, 음식 등이 어울리다, 잘 맞다

② **guts**(=nerve)

I don't have the guts to tell him what I really think.

나는 그에게 내가 진짜로 생각하는 것을 말할 배짱이 없어.

③ **get away from**

You can't get away from this. You know how mom doesn't like us to lie.

너 이번엔 반드시 혼날 거야. 너 엄마가 우리가 거짓말하는 걸 얼마나 싫어하는지 알지

☑ get away from: 잘못한 것 등으로부터 빠져나가다

Day 201

① get caught in the rain

A: Did you get caught in the rain on the way here?
B: Luckily, no, I had my umbrella with me.

A: 올 때 비 맞았니?
B: 아니, 다행히 우산이 있었어.

☑ get caught in traffic: (차량이 많아) 길이 막히다
get caught with work: 일이 많다

② give in

My niece kept pestering for candy and I gave in.

우리 조카가 사탕 사달라고 계속 졸라대서 결국 내가 졌지.

☑ give in: 굴복하다, 항복하다
give up: 포기하다(하던 것을)

③ grab

A: Are you ready?
B: I'll just grab my things and off we go.

A: 준비 다했어?
B: 내 물건 좀 챙기고 그리고 가자.

☑ grab my [cell phone/jacket …]: 집어 들다, 챙기다

Day 202

① go for a walk

Before I go for a walk I need to get changed. (= change my clothes)

산책 나가기 전에 옷을 갈아입어야해.

☑ go for [a run/a swim …]

② get into a habit of

You should get into the habit of thinking and speaking in English.

너는 영어로 생각하고 말하는 습관을 들여야 해.

= make it a habit to think and speak

③ go on and on

He went on and on about his dogs.

그는 그의 개에 대해서 쉴 새 없이 계속 얘기했어.

☑ go on and on: (지루하게 긴 시간)계속하다

- The movie went on and on.

Day 203

① get back

Let's get back to the topic later on.

그 주제에 대해서는 나중에 다시 말하자!

☑ get back: 돌아오다 / 가다

- What time did you get back? 너 몇 시에 돌아왔니?

② get st across

I think I should learn to speak well. I find it hard to get my point across to others.

나는 말을 잘하는 방법을 배워야할 것 같아. 다른 사람들에게 내 얘기를 전달하는 것이 힘들어.

☑ get st across: 다른 사람을 이해시키다

③ get the hang of st

I didn't know how to ride a bike but After several falls, I got the hang of it.

난 자전거를 탈줄 몰랐는데 몇 번 넘어지고 나서 감을 잡았어.

☑ get the hang of something: (무언가를 반복해서 함으로써) 감을 잡다

learn the ropes: (훈련이나 배움의 과정을 통해) 요령을 익히다

Day 204

① go off

My alarm clock didn't go off so I was late for school.

알람이 안 울려서 학교에 지각했어.

☑ go off: 울리다(소리가 나다)

☑ The light wen off. 불이 나가다

② get at

What are you getting at?

무슨 말을 하려는 거니?

☑ get at: 뜻하다, 함축하다, 내포하다

- I don't understand what you're getting at. 무슨 말인지 이해가 안 돼.

③ go away

It's been more than a week but this bruise hasn't gone away.

일주일이 넘었는데 이 멍이 안 없어졌어.

☑ go away: 없어지다 / 사라지다 / 떠나다

- The stain didn't go away. 얼룩이 안 없어졌어.
- Let's go away somewhere warm and nice.
  따뜻하고 좋은 곳으로 여행가자!

Day 205

① **have plans**

I have plans with my friend this afternoon.

나 오늘 오후에 친구랑 약속이 있어.

☑ Do you have any plans for the weekend? 주말에 계획 있니?

② **have a hard time**

Did you have a hard time solving that problem?

그 문제 푸느라 힘들었니?

= have trouble+동사ing: ~ 하느라 힘든 시간을 보내다, 고생을 하다

③ **How did it go**

I heard you took part in a dance competition. How did it go?

너 댄스 경연대회에 참가했었다며? 어떻게 됐어?

Day 206

① **humid**

Summer in Korea is hot and humid.

한국의 여름은 덥고 습해.

② **a hassle**

I know I should floss after brushing my teeth but it's such a hassle.

칫솔질 후에 치실 질을 해야 하는 건 아는데 너무 귀찮아.

☑ a hassle: 번거로움

③ **hang out**

I usually hang out with my friends on weekends.

나는 주말에 보통 친구들과 놀아.

☑ hang out: 시간을 보내다

· I just hung out at home. 나 그냥 집에 있었어. (집에서 시간을 보냈다)

Day 207

① **have in common**

We have a lot in common.

우리는 공통점이 많아.

☑ we have nothing in common. 우리는 공통점이 없어.

② **have a lesson**

I had a piano lesson before this class.

이 수업 전에 피아노 수업을 받았어요.

☑ I'm going to take a yoga class(lesson) from next week.
나 다음 주부터 요가 수업 받을 거야.

③ **hold on**(=Hang on/Wait)

Hold on! I'm gonna get my pen.

잠깐 기다려봐! 볼펜 좀 가져올게.

Day 208

① **hand in**(=turn in)

A: When is it due?

B: I've got to hand in tomorrow.

A: 그거 언제까지야?

B: 내일까지 제출해야해.

② **hand out**(=give out(around)/pass out(around))

There were a couple of people handing out fliers on the way to the subway station.

전철역 가는 길에 전단지를 나눠주는 사람들이 몇 명 있었어.

☑ hand out: 나눠주다, 배포하다

③ **hands down**

He is hands down the best soccer player ever.

그는 단연코 역대 최고의 축구선수야.

Day 209

① st+hurt

My legs hurt.

다리 아파.

☑ It hurts. 아파.

☑ hurt - hurt - hurt

② sb+hurt

I hurt my finger.

나 손가락 다쳤어.

☑ She got hurt her arm. 그녀는 팔을 다쳤어.

☑ · Are(Were) you hurt? 너 다쳤니?

· Did you get hurt? 너 다쳤니?

· Does it hurt? 아프니?

③ have no idea

You have no idea how scary it is.

그게 얼마나 무서운지 넌 상상도 안 될 거야.

Day 210

① **Having said that**(= (with) that said)

I'm terrible at remembering people's names. Having said that, I'm not bad when it comes to remembering names of flowers.

난 사람들 이름을 정말 잘 못 외워. 근데 그렇게 말은 했지만 꽃 이름들을 외우는 건 또 잘해.

☑ 앞의 말과 반대되는 말을 할 때

② **have a blast**

I had a blast at the amusement park enjoying lots of exciting rides.

나 놀이공원에서 여러 가지 재미있는 놀이기구를 타면서 정말 신나게 놀았어.

③ **have+sb+동사원형**

First period, my korean class, my teacher had us write poems.

1교시 국어시간에는 시를 썼어. (선생님이 우리한테 시를 쓰게 하셨어).

☑ have+sb+동사원형: 누구를 ~하게 하다 (일, 책임감 등을 주다)

Day 211

① happen to

Do you happen to know a person called Bob?

너 혹시 밥이라는 사람 아니?

② have a long way to go

A: Your English is excellent.

B: Thanks, but I have a long way to go.

A: 너 영어 정말 잘한다.

B: 고마워, 근데 나 아직 멀었어.

③ have nothing to do with

A: Who ate my pizza?

B: Why are you looking at me? I have nothing to do with it.

A: 누가 내 피자먹었어?

B: 왜 날 쳐다보는 건데. 나랑 상관없거든.

☑ What does it have to do with me? 그게 나랑 무슨 상관이야?

Day 212

① hold on to

Hold on to your dreams! If you don't give up you're bound to make it.

너의 꿈을 놓치마! 네가 포기하지 않으면 너는 너의 꿈을 이룰 수밖에 없어.

☑ hold on to [the rope/the job …] ~을 붙잡다(물리적/추상적)

② have mixed feelings

I have mixed feelings about getting older.

나이가 드는 게 좋기도 하고 나쁘기도 해.

③ have come a long way

칠득, your English has come a long way. You didn't even understand 'breakfast' when I first met you.

칠득아 너 영어 많이 발전했다. 내가 너를 처음 만났을 때 너 'breakfast'조차 몰랐잖아.

Day 213

① have the upper hand

Check out the guy! He is much taller and bigger than the other guy. He definitely has the upper hand.

저 사람 좀 봐! 상대방보다 훨씬 더 키가 크고 몸집도 커. 그가 확실히 더 유리해.

① homebody

He's a homebody. Unless it's absolutely necessary he won't come out of his place.

그는 집에 있는 것을 좋아해. 정말 필요할 때 아니면 집에서 안 나올 거야.

☑ homebody: 집돌이, 집순이

③ hit the nail on the head(=exactly)

A: All I need is have more confidence?

B: You hit the nail on the head.

A: 내게 필요한 건 자신감을 더 갖는 거라고?

B: 딱 맞혔어.

Day 214

① **hold your horses**

Hold your horses! I haven't finished it yet.

흥분하지 마! 나 아직 안 끝났어.

☑ hold your horses: 상대가 침착하지 않고 호들갑을 떨 때

② **head to**(=go to)

We headed to the train station after lunch.

우리는 점심 먹고 기차역으로 갔어.

☑ head [out/toward/up/down …]

③ **have no choice but**

I had no choice but to listen to what my mom said.

우리엄마 말을 들을 수밖에 없었어.

Day 215

① hundreds of

Hundreds of people were there to see the famous boy band.

수많은 사람들이 그 유명한 보이그룹을 보기위해 거기에 있었어.

② hold sb back

A: What holds you back to become a singer?

B: My stage fright.

A: 뭐가 널 가수가 되는 것을 막고 있니?

B: 나의 무대공포증.

☑ hold+sb+back: 망설이게 하다, 주저하게 하다

③ hit it off

We hit it off right away and became best friends.

우리는 바로 잘 맞았고 제일 친한 친구가 되었지.

☑ hit it off: 처음부터 바로 잘 맞다, 바로 친해지다

Day 216

① **hang in there**(=tough it out)

Hang in there! You know 'This too shall pass'.

힘들겠지만 참고 버텨! 이것 또한 지나가리라 알지.

☑ My first year in college was hard but I toughed it out and finished with good grades.
대학 일학년 때 힘들었는데 참고 버텨서 좋은 성적으로 마무리했어.

② **hesitate**

Don't hesitate to ask any question!

망설이지 말고 어떤 질문이라도 해!

= Don't be hesitant …

☑ hesitate: 주저하다/망설이다

③ **hold a grudge**

He's not the person who holds a grudge. He's very cool.

그는 오래 동안 삐쳐있고 그런 사람이 아니야. 그는 성격이 좋아.

☑ hold a grudge: 나쁜 감정을 오래 담아두다, 꽁해있다

Day 217

① have a fight

I had a fight with my brother yesterday. Even though I still think it's his fault I said sorry.

어제 남동생하고 싸웠어. 그게 걔 잘못이라고 아직 생각하지만 미안하다고 했어.

☑ have a fight: 다투다, 싸우다

② hang up

You can hang up your jacket on the hook.

저 고리에 재킷을 걸어놔.

☑ hang up: 걸다, 걸어놓다/전화를 끊다

③ help yourself

Help yourself!

마음껏 드세요!

☑ · Help yourself to these snacks on the table.
탁자위에 있는 간식 맘대로 드세요!
· Help yourself to the stationery. 그 문구류들 맘대로 사용하세요!

Day 218

① **-ish**

The cat was kind of brownish.

그 고양이는 갈색 같은 색깔이었어.

☑ reddish 불그스름한 / sevenish 일곱 시 정도

② **It's 형 of+sb**

It was kind of you to give up your seat to the old lady.

할머니께 자리를 양보하다니 넌 참 친절 하구나.

☑ It is [nice/sweet/mean …] of+sb

③ **in that case**

In that case, I'll just have pizza.

그렇다면, 나는 그냥 피자 먹을래.

Day 219

① **if possible**

If possible, I'd love to go to England this year.

가능하다면, 난 올해 영국에 가고 싶어.

② **in time**

I was able to get to the airport just in time for my flight.

나는 겨우 비행기시간에 늦지 않게 공항에 도착할 수 있었어.

☑ in time: 제시간에/약속된 시간 전에
on time: 정각에

③ **in trouble**

I should go home now or else I'll be in trouble.

나 지금 집에 가야해 그렇지 않으면 혼날 거야(곤경에 빠지다).

Day 220

① **I think**

I think I should read more books.

내 생각에 나는 더 많은 책을 읽어야 할 것 같아.

② **I don't think**

I don't think it's going to rain today.

내 생각에 오늘 비 안 올 것 같은데.

☑ I don't think: ~하지 않을 것 같아

③ **I mean**

I mean it's possible but it takes time.

내말은 그게 가능은 하지만 시간이 걸린다는 뜻이야.

Day 221

① I feel

I felt so good after cleaning up my room.

내 방 청소 후에 기분이 아주 좋았어.

☑ feel - felt - felt

② I'm sure

I'm sure she'll like your present.

나는 그녀가 너의 선물을 좋아할 거라고 확신해.

③ I'm thinking of

I'm thinking of getting a new cell phone.

나 새 핸드폰을 사려고 생각중이야.

Day 222

① **I'm sorry**

I'm sorry you didn't have anyone to talk to.

말할 상대가 아무도 없었다니 유감이야.

☑ I'm sorry: 안됐다

- I'm sorry to hear that. 그것을 듣게 되어 유감이네요

② **I hope**

I hope this book will help you improve your English.

이 책이 너의 영어에 도움이 되길 바라.

③ **I guess**

I guess he is busy.

그가 바쁜가봐.

☑ I guess: 내 생각/추측은

Day 223

① **I'm afraid**

I'm afraid I'm not able to make it on Saturday.

정말 죄송한데 토요일에 못갈 것 같아요.

☑ I'm afraid: 죄송하지만, 유감스럽지만

② **I bet**

I bet you can beat him easily.

내가 장담하는데 너는 그를 쉽게 이길 수 있어.

③ **I was wondering if**

I was wondering if I could use this.

혹시 제가 이것을 사용해도 될까요?

☑ 공손하게 물어볼 때

Day 224

① **I heard**

I heard 칠득 is going to move to 제주도 next month.

칠득이 다음 달에 제주도로 이사 간대.

☑ I heard: ~래/내가 들었는데

② **in a row**

I love 청국장. I can eat 청국장 for five days in a row.

나 청국장 정말 좋아. 나는 청국장을 5일 내내 먹을 수 있어.

③ **in person**

Have you ever seen any celebrities in person?

너는 유명인사를 실제로 본 적 있니?

☑ in person: 실제로, 직접

Day 225

① in charge of

My dad used to be in charge of the bathroom but now I clean up the bathroom.

우리 아빠가 화장실 담당이었는데 지금은 내가 청소해.

☑ in charge of: ~를 담당하는

- Who's in charge? 누가 담당이지?

② It's time

It's time to say goodbye to your old self.

너의 예전의 모습과 이별을 할 시간이야.

☑ It's time for+명사

③ It's just that

A: You don't look too good today.

B: It's just that I didn't get to bed as early.

A: 너 오늘 별로 안 좋아 보인다.

B: 그냥 어제 일찍 못 자서 그래.

Day 226

① It's not that

It's not that I don't like spicy food but I prefer sweet foods.

내가 매운 음식을 싫어 한다는 게 아니고 난 단 음식을 더 좋아한다고.

☑ It's not that: ~해서가 아니야

② in the back of one's mind

칠자 always makes fun of her brother 칠득 but in the back of her mind, she really cares about him.

칠자는 늘 그녀의 오빠인 칠득이를 놀려대지만 마음속으로는 그를 정말 생각해.

③ in one sitting

I used to eat more than ten tangerines in one sitting in the winter time when I was little.

나는 어렸을 때 겨울이면 한자리에서 귤을 열 개 넘게 먹곤 했어.

Day 227

① in terms of

In terms of your speaking, there's only one way to improve it. Speak!

말하기 실력에 있어서는, 그것을 향상시킬 수 있는 방법은 하나밖에 없어. 말해!

② in fact

It was okay. In fact it was boring. I kept yawning during the movie.

그냥 그랬어. 실은 재미없었어. 영화 보는 동안 나는 계속 하품했어.

③ It happens

It's okay. It happens.

괜찮아. 그럴 수도 있지

☑ It happens: 종종 일어나는 일이야

Day 228

① **in no time**

When I feel down, I always listen to this music. It makes me feel good in no time.

나는 기분이 울적할 때 항상 이 음악을 들어. 그게 나를 금방 기분 좋게 해줘.

② **in the mean time**

The movie starts at two. So in the mean time why don't we grab a bite to eat?

그 영화가 두시에 시작해. 그러니까 그동안 우리 뭐 좀 먹자.

☑ in the mean time: 다른 뭔가를 기다리는 동안

☑ for the time being 당분간은

③ **it's … that ~**

A: I really look up to 이순신. He created this beautiful 한글.

B: 칠득! It's 세종대왕 that made 한글.

A: 나 진짜 이순신을 존경해. 그는 이 아름다운 한글을 창제하셨잖아.

B: 칠득아, 한글을 만든 건 세종대왕이야.

☑ it's … that ~ : ~는 … 이다

- It was Saturday that we ate 떡볶이.
  우리가 떡볶이를 먹은 것은 토요일이었어.

Day 229

① **I can't believe**

I can't believe It's already December.

벌써 12월이라니 믿을 수가 없어.

② **Is it because**

Is it because you don't have time?

네가 시간이 없어서 그러니?

③ **indulge in**(=indulge myself)

It's a cheat day. I'm going to indulge in lots of foods.

오늘은 치팅데이야. 많은 음식을 마음껏 먹을 거야.

☑ indulge in: 마음껏 즐기다

Day 230

① in a+형용사+manner

I think he was a bit rude. He could've said in a more civil manner.

나는 그가 예의가 좀 없었다고 생각 해. 그는 좀 더 정중하게 말할 수 있었어.

☑ in a 형용사 manner: 한 방법으로, 방식으로

- in an effective manner 효과적인 방법으로

☑ in a … [manner/fashion/way]

② invest in

You should invest your time and effort in practicing English to be a good English speaker.

네가 영어짱이 되려면 너의 시간과 노력을 영어 연습하는데 투자해야 해.

☑ invest in: ~에 투자하다

③ in case(=just in case)

Why don't you bring your jacket in case the weather gets cold?

날씨가 추워질 때를 대비해서 재킷을 가져가지 그러니?

Day 231

① in the first place

You shouldn't have bought them in the first place.

네가 애초에 그것들을 사지 말았어야지.

② in mind

What shall we have for lunch? Do you have something in mind?

우리 점심으로 뭐 먹을까? 뭐 생각해둔 거 있니?

☑ ··· a person in mind 생각해둔 사람

··· a place in mind 생각해둔 장소

☑ I have a lot on my mind these days. 나 요즘에 머리가 좀 복잡해.

③ It's not rocket science

First of all, put it in the microwave and then press this button. It's not rocket science.

먼저 그걸 전자레인지에 넣어. 그리고 나서 이 버튼을 눌러. 어렵지 않잖아.

Day 232

① If it weren't for

If it weren't for your advice, I wouldn't be where I am right now.

너의 조언이 아니었다면 나는 지금 이 자리에 없을 거야.

② It would be great if

It would be great if we could go anywhere we want without a passport or a visa.

여권이나 비자 없이 우리가 원하는 곳을 어디든지 갈 수 있다면 정말 좋겠다.

③ in the past

There was no game console, not to mention computers or cell phones in the past.

옛날에는 컴퓨터, 핸드폰은 말할 것도 없고 게임기도 없었어.

Day 233

① It's no surprise

It's no surprise they're popular. they're good singers, dancers and most of all, they're warm hearted people.

그들이 인기 있는 것도 당연해. 그들은 노래도 잘하지, 춤도 잘 추지 그리고 무엇보다도 좋은 인성을 가지고 있잖아.

② It's not a big deal

It's just a sty. It's not a big deal. It'll heal itself.

그냥 눈 다래끼 일뿐이야. 별거 아니야. 저절로 나을 거야.

↔ It's a big deal. 중요한, 대단한 일이야.

③ It's no use 동사ing

It's no use complaining about the weather.

날씨에 대해 불평해봤자 소용없어.

Day 234

① **in someone's shoes**

It's almost impossible to be totally in someone's shoes. However we should at least try to understand what the other person is going through.

완전히 누군가의 입장이 되어 생각하는 것은 거의 불가능해. 하지만 적어도 상대방의 상황을 이해하려고 노력은 해야 해.

② **in the middle of**

I was in the middle of something.

나 뭔가 하고 있는 중이었어.

☑ The building is in the middle of nowhere.(외딴곳)

☑ in the middle of the night 한밤중

② **in bulk**

If you buy it in bulk you'll get a discount.

네가 그것을 다량으로 구매하면 할인을 받을 거야.

Day 235

① **in that**

I'm so lucky in that I have a job that I love so much and I'm best at.

내가 정말 좋아하고 잘하는 것을 나의 직업으로 가지고 있다는 점에서 나는 정말 운이 좋은 사람이야.

② **I don't know about you but**

I don't know about you but I need seven to eight hours of sleep at night or else it's hard to function properly the next day.

넌 어떤지 모르겠지만 난 밤에 7시간이나 8시간정도는 자야지 그렇지 않으면 그 다음날 힘들어.

③ **I don't know what to say**

Wow, What's this? You remember my birthday. I don't know what to say.

와우, 이게 뭐야? 너 내 생일 기억하는구나. 내가 뭐라고 말해야할지 모르겠다.

Day 236

① identify with

I truly enjoyed the movie because I could identify with all the characters in it.

그 영화에 나오는 모든 등장인물들에게 공감할 수 있었기 때문에 나는 그 영화를 정말 재밌게 봤어.

☑ identify with: 동일시하다

☑ can relate to: 공감하다

② in half

Cut the apple in half and take the seeds out.

사과를 반으로 자르고 씨들을 빼.

③ in the mood for

I'm in the mood for chinese food today.

나는 오늘 중국음식이 땡겨.

☑ in the mood for: ~를 원하다

☑ in the mood for [dancing/a movie]

in the mood to [dance/talk about]

Day 237

① **in a way**

In a way, he is right. We should do what we need to do.

어느 면에서는 그가 옳아. 우리는 우리가 해야 할 일을 해야 해.

② **in general**

In general, girls like pink and boys like blue.

일반적으로 여자아이들은 분홍색을 좋아하고 남자아이들은 파란색을 좋아해.

③ **I love it when**

I love it when I hear birds chirping the moment I wake up.

잠에서 깰 때 새소리를 듣는 것을 정말 좋아해.

☑ I love it when: ~일 때/할 때 좋아

↔ I hate it when

Day 238

① **in the end**

In the end, it's up to you to choose what to do.

결국엔 무엇을 할까 선택하는 것은 너한테 달렸어.

② **in advance**(=beforehand)

If you want to change the time, let me know in advance.

만약에 시간을 바꾸고 싶으면 나에게 미리 알려줘.

③ **in a nutshell**

In a nutshell, it was the best movie ever.

한마디로, 역대 최고의 영화였어.

Day 239

① just in case

I'll take my wallet with me just in case.

혹시 모르니까 지갑 가져가야겠어.

② jealous

A: I'm going to South Africa.

B: I'm jealous.

A: 나 남아프리카에 가.

B: 부럽다~.

☑ jealous of+[st/sb]

③ just about

칠득 is good at fixing things. He can fix just about anything and everything.

칠득이는 물건들을 잘 고쳐. 그는 거의 모든 것을 고칠 수 있어.

Day 240

① just because~ doesn't mean

Just because one lives in an English speaking country it doesn't mean that he or she is a fluent English speaker.

어떤 사람이 영어권 나라에 산다고 해서 그 혹은 그녀가 영어를 잘한다는 의미는 아니야.

② jump out at

As soon as I walked into the place, the fantabulous chandelier jumped out at me.

거기에 들어서자마자 정말 멋진 샹들리에가 눈에 확 들어왔어.

③ jam-packed

The subway was jam-packed. I almost missed my stop.

전철이 사람들로 꽉 차서 내 정류장에서 못 내릴 뻔했어.

☑ jam-packed with [people/interesting facts …]: (사람, 사물 등)~로 꽉 찬

Day 241

① **jot down**(=write down/note down/put down)

Jot down the words and expressions you don't know and look them up.

네가 모르는 단어랑 표현들을 써놔 그리고 뜻을 찾아봐.

② **jump into**

Let's jump into today's topic!

우리 오늘 주제를 빨리 시작하자!

☑ jump into water. 물에 뛰어들다.

③ **jaywalk**

Don't jaywalk! It's dangerous.

무단횡단하지 마! 위험해.

Day 242

① keep+동사ing

He is very talkative. He keeps talking.

그는 말이 정말 많아. 그는 계속 말해.

= He goes on and on.

☑ keep (on) [eating/reading/silent …]

② keep up

Keep up the good work!

지금까지처럼 앞으로도 잘해라!

☑ keep up: 지금 하는 것처럼 계속하다

- Keep this pace up and you'll make it. 지금처럼 하면 넌 성공할거야.

③ keep A away from B

This one will keep mosquitoes away from you.

이게 너에게서 모기를 쫓아줄 거야.

☑ keep A away from B: A를 B로 부터 쫓아내다

Day 243

① know inside out

Ask Kim! He knows that stuff inside out

김한테 물어봐! 그가 그런 거에 전문가야.

☑ know inside out: 무언가에 대해서 매우 잘 알다

② keep up with

It was hard to keep up with my schoolwork after traveling around Europe with my family for two months.

가족들과 두 달 동안 유럽여행을 갔다 온 후에 학교수업을 따라가기가 정말 힘들었어.

☑ Can you slow down! I can't keep up with you.
천천히 좀 가! 내가 따라갈 수가 없다.

③ keep in touch with

It's hard to keep in touch with old friends.

옛 친구들과 계속 연락하고 지내는 것은 힘들어.

Day 244

① **kick the habit**(=break a habit)

How did you kick the habit of biting your nails?

너 손톱을 물어뜯는 습관을 어떻게 버렸니?

② **kick off**

The game kicks off at seven p.m.

그 게임은 저녁 7시에 시작해.

③ **Keep your chin up!**(=Chin up)

Keep your chin up! Things will get better soon.

힘내! 곧 다 좋아질 거야.

Day 245

① **look at**

Stop looking at your cell phone!

핸드폰 좀 그만 봐!

☑ look at: ~을 보다

☑ look into: ~을 들여다보다/알아보다, 조사하다

② **look forward to**

I'm so looking forward to going on a safari in Africa.

아프리카로 사파리를 떠나는 때를 고대하고 있어.

③ **like I said**(=as I said)

Like I said, I don't enjoy wearing accessories except for the occasions.

내가 말했듯이 특별한 때를 제외하곤 난 악세사리를 즐기지 않아.

Day 246

① **look for**

A: What are you doing?

B: I'm looking for the spatular. Oh, I found it.

A: 너 뭐해?

B: 뒤집개 찾고 있어. 아 찾았다.

② **look up**

Why don't you look it up on the internet?

인터넷에서 찾아보지 그러니?

☑ look up: 모르는 단어, 정보를 찾아보다

☑ Why don't you look up the word in a dictionary?
그 단어를 사전에서 찾아보지 그러니?

③ **look up to**(=respect)

Who do you look up to?

네가 존경하는 사람은 누구야?

Day 247

① lose weight

I'm trying to lose weight but it's harder than I thought.

나 살을 빼려고 하는데 생각보다 더 힘들어.

☑ lose weight: 살을 빼다, 체중을 줄이다

☑ lose ~~my~~ weight → lose some weight

↔ put on weight 살이 찌다

② let go

Don't let go of the balloon! Hold it tight!

풍선 놓치마! 꽉 잡아!

☑ let go: 잡았던 것을 놓다, 놔주다, 나쁜 일을 잊다, 떨쳐내다, 보내다

☑ I'll let go of all my worries and just chill.
모든 걱정들을 잊고 그냥 편하게 쉴 거야.

③ leave out

I've been to France, Germany, Italy, and Finland. Oh, I left out England.

나는 프랑스, 독일, 이탈리아 그리고 핀란드에 가봤어. 아 영국을 빼먹었네.

☑ leave out: -를/을 포함하지 않다, 밖에 놓아두다

☑ feel left out: 소외감을 느끼다

Day 248

① last

My old phone didn't last long after charging. That's why I got a new one.

내 옛날 전화는 충전 후에 오래 가질 않았어. 그래서 내가 새 거 산거야.

☑ last: 지속되다

☑ last night: 어젯밤

the last night of the camping: 캠핑의 마지막 밤

② let sb down

I'm sorry to let you down. I promise I won't do it again.

내가 너를 실망시켜서 미안해. 다시는 안 그럴게 약속해.

☑ let sb down: ~을(를)실망시키다

③ Let's say(=say)

Let's say there were only two countries, hot and cold, where would you like to live?

더운 나라, 추운 나라, 두 나라밖에 없다고 치자(가정하자), 넌 어디에 살고 싶니?

Day 249

① **live up to**

The movie didn't live up to my expectations.

그 영화는 내 기대에 못 미쳤어.

☑ live up to: 기대에 미치다, 부응하다

② **long story short**

Long story short, we lost the game.

짧게 말해서, 우리가 게임에서 졌어.

☑ long story short: 간단히 말해서

③ **let alone**

I didn't have time for water, let alone lunch.

나 점심은커녕 물 마실 시간도 없었어.

Day 250

① likely

If you just keep learning new words and don't review what you've learned, you'll likely forget most of them.

네가 만약에 계속 새로운 단어만 배우고 배운 것을 복습하지 않는다면 너는 대부분의 것들을 잃어버리게 될 거야.

☑ likely: 할 확률이 높은, 가 예상이 되는

② look in the mirror

What? What did you say? Looking in the mirror? There's no mirror there.

뭐? 너 뭐라고 했니? 거울을 보면서? 거기 거울 없는데….

☑ look in the mirror: 거울을 보다

③ local

김치찌개? in Italy? Don't you think we should try local food.

김치찌개? 이탈리아에서? 현지음식을 먹어봐야 한다고 생각되지 않니?

☑ local food: 현지음식, 그 지역음식

☑ local [people/time/shops …]

Day 251

① **listen to**

Not many people listen to the radio nowadays.

요즘엔 라디오를 듣는 사람이 많지 않아.

☑ listen to [music/your parents …]

② **look after**(=take care of)

If you go on a trip to 제주도 who's going to look after your cats?

네가 제주도로 여행을 가면 누가 너의 고양이들을 돌봐?

☑ look after: 돌보다

③ **look out** (of)

Look out (of) the window! It's snowing.

창밖을 봐! 눈이 오고 있어.

☑ Look out! 조심해!

Day 252

① looking around

A: Can I help you with something?

B: I'm just looking (around).

A: 도와드릴까요?

B: 그냥 둘러보는 중이에요.

= I'm just browsing.

② look back

I thought it was very hard back then but when I look back on it now it wasn't that bad.

그때는 그게 힘들었다고 생각했는데 지금 돌아보면 그렇게 나쁘지만은 않았던 것 같아.

☑ look back: 과거를 돌이켜보다

③ lie down

I usually watch TV lying down on the couch.

나는 텔레비전을 볼 때 보통 소파에 누워서 봐.

☑ lie down: 눕다

lay down: 누워 있었다

Day 253

① **look down on**

Don't look down on people who drive compact cars.

소형차를 운전하는 사람들을 무시하지 마!

☑ look down on: 무시하다, 깔보다

② **let**(=allow+sb+to 동사원형)

let me show you how to do this.

내가 이거 어떻게 하는 건지 보여줄게.

☑ let: ~하게 하다(허락하다) / ~하게 시키다

My parents don't let me go out at night.
우리 부모님은 내가 밤에 나가는 것을 허락하지 않으셔.

③ **let one's guard down**

Until we're absolutely free from this covid-19, we shouldn't let our guard down.

우리가 이 코로나로부터 완전히 해방되지 전까지는 방심하면 안 돼.

☑ let one's guard down: 방심하다

Day 254

① **last but not least**

Last but not least, you should love what you do.

마지막으로(하지만 앞에 말한 것들만큼 중요한), 너는 네가 하는 일을 좋아해야 해.

② **lighten up**

Lighten up! Your grades are not everything.

얼굴 좀 펴! 성적이 다가 아니잖아.

☑ lighten up: 너무 심각하게 받아들이지 마 / 밝게 하다, 분위기를 띄우다

③ **lead to**

If you only sit and not move around a lot it'll lead to health problems

네가 그냥 앉아만 있고 많이 움직이지 않으면 그게 건강문제로 이어질 거야.

☑ lead to: ~로 이어지다, 이르게 하다, 야기하다

Day 255

① mean

A: What does 짱 mean?
B: It means 'the best'.

A: 짱이 무슨 뜻이야?
B: 그것은 최고라는 의미야.

☑ I mean …. 내 말은 ….

② make sense

It doesn't make any sense at all. You were hungry so you didn't eat lunch?

말이 전혀 안되잖아. 네가 배가 고파서 점심을 안 먹었다고?

☑ make sense: 말이 되다, 이해가 되다

③ mull st over(=sleep on it)

I think I need some time to mull it over.

나에게 그것에 대해 곰곰이 생각할 시간이 필요해.

☑ mull st over: 시간을 두고 깊이 생각하다
mull over [the idea/life/options …]

Day 256

① **more or less**

I think this one is more or less the same as the one we saw just before.

내 생각에는 이거 조금 전에 우리가 본 거하고 거의 똑같은데.

② **make it**

Someday I want to say "I've made it to be an excellent English speaker.

언젠가 "난 영어짱이 되었어!"라고 말하고 싶어.

☑ make it: ~해내다, 성공하다

- make it at 2: 2시에 만날 수 있다
- make it on Friday: 금요일에 갈수 있다
- make it to the top: 정상까지 오를 수 있다

③ **get a mosquito bite**

A: How did you sleep?

B: I couldn't sleep well because of mosquitoes. Look! I got several mosquito bites.

A: 잘 잤니?

B: 모기 때문에 잘 못 잤어. 봐! 나 몇 군데 모기에 물렸어.

Day 257

① make up

Did you make up that story? That sounds like a true story.

그 얘기 네가 만들어 낸 거야? 진짜 있었던 얘기처럼 들려.

☑ make up: 이야기를 지어내다 / 차지하다 / 화장품

☑ make up for: 만회하다, 보충하다

make up with+sb: ~와 화해하다

② mess with

Don't mess with my dog when sleeping. she can be very aggressive.

우리 강아지 잘 때 건드리지 마. 굉장히 사나워져.

☑ mess with: 장난치다, 건들다

☑ mess up: 망치다

③ mind goes blank

Someone asked me for directions in English today and my mind went blank. I couldn't use any of the words or expressions I learned.

오늘 누가 나한테 영어로 길을 물어봤는데 머리가 하얘지더라고. 내가 배운 단어들과 표현들을 하나도 못 써먹었어.

Day 258

① **make do**

A: Spinach is the only thing we have in the fridge right now.

B: We've got to make do with what we have.

A: 냉장고에 지금 시금치밖에 없는데.

B: 있는 걸로 대충 때우지 뭐.

② **more often than not**

More often than not, if you say 'sorry' the other person accepts your apology.

보통 네가 미안하다고하면 상대방은 너의 사과를 받아줘.

③ **mix up**

A: It's 세종대왕 that made 한글, not 이순신.

B: Oh! I mixed up.

A: 한글을 만드신 분은 세종대왕이야 이순신 장군이 아니고.

B: 아! 내가 착각했어.

☑ mix up: A와 B를 혼동하다, 착각하다

☑ • He's(is) mistaken. 그의 착각이야.

• I must have been mistaken. 내가 착각했나봐.

Day 259

① **make one's mouth water**

The smell of the food makes my mouth water.

그 음식 냄새가 입안에 군침을 돌게 해.

☑ make my eyes water: 눈물이 나다

② **move out**

We're moving out in two weeks. We're moving to 제주도.

우리 2주후에 이사가. 제주도로 이사가.

☑ move out: 이사 가다(살던, 일하던 곳에서 나가다)

③ **miss out on**

Don't miss out on this opportunity to taste my mom's amazing cooking.

우리엄마의 훌륭한 음식을 맛볼 기회를 놓치지 마!

☑ miss out on: 좋은 기회, 경험을 놓치다

☑ miss: 놓치다, 피하다, 그리워하다

Day 260

① **make an exception**

Could you make an exception for this?

이것은 예외로 해주세요!

② **move on**

Let's move on to the next topic!

다음 주제로 넘어가자!

③ **make concessions**(=give up, let, yield)

It was me that made concessions last time and the last time.

지난번 그리고 지지난번에도 양보를 한 건 나였어.

☑ make concessions: 양보하다

Day 261

① **make breakfast**(=cook breakfast)

While my mom was making dinner, I did my homework.

엄마가 저녁식사를 준비하는 동안 난 숙제를 했어.

☑ make [breakfast/lunch/떡볶이 …]: 식사, 음식을 만들다 / 요리하다

② **make sure**

I'll make sure to memorize three sentences a day.

나는 하루에 세 문장씩 꼭 외울 거야.

☑ make sure: 확실히 하다

- Make sure that you review what you've learned.
  반드시 네가 배운 것을 복습하도록 해.

③ **make the most of+st**

Life is short. We should make the most of our precious time.

인생은 짧아. 우리는 최대한 우리의 귀중한 시간을 성실히 살아내야 해.

☑ make the most of+st: ~를 알차게 쓰다, 보내다

Day 262

① more and more

More and more people enjoy traveling abroad.

점점 더 많은 사람들이 해외여행을 즐겨.

↔ less and less

② make a wish

Make wishes before you blow the candles!

촛불을 끄기 전에 소원을 빌어!

③ measure up

You'd better measure (up) before you cut it out.

그거 자르기 전에 재보는 게 좋을걸.

☑ measure up: 치수를 측정하다, 재보다

☑ measure up (to): 어떤 기준에 적합하다, 부합하다

Day 263

① **make a mistake**

Don't be afraid of making mistakes when you speak English!

영어로 말할 때 실수하는 것을 두려워하지 마!

☑ make a mistake: 실수하다

② **mindlessly**

I hate it when people mindlessly throw their trash away on the street.

난 사람들이 아무생각 없이 길에 쓰레기를 버리는 게 정말 싫어.

③ **make one's day**

Thank you for the message! You made my day!

문자 고마워! 덕분에 행복한 날이 되었어.

Day 264

① **not at all**

I'll skip lunch. I'm not hungry at all.

나 점심 안 먹을래(건너뛰다). 나 배가 하나도(전혀) 안고파.

② **no matter+w의문사**

No one can solve this problem no matter how smart they are.

아무도 이 문제를 풀 수 없어 그들이 아무리 똑똑해도.

☑ no matter [what/who/where …]

③ **no one**

No one likes selfish people.

아무도 이기적인 사람을 좋아하지 않아.

☑ Not every korean likes 김치. 모든 한국인이 다 김치를 좋아하는 것은 아니야.

Day 265

① now that

Now that you know how to make English sentences, you should learn as many words and expressions as possible from now.

너는 이제 영어문장들을 만드는 방법을 알고 있으니 지금부터는 가능한 한 많은 단어와 표현들을 익혀야해.

☑ now that: 이제 ~이니까

② necessary

Is it necessary to know that word?

그 단어를 알 필요가 있을까?

☑ necessary: 필요한

③ name after

The street was named after a famous singer.

그 길의 이름은 유명한 가수의 이름을 따서 지어졌어.

= They named the street after the renowned singer.

Day 266

① No way

A: Can I use your toothbrush?
B: What? No way! That's disgusting.

A: 너 칫솔 좀 써도 되니?
B: 뭐? 말도 안 되는 소리하고 있네. 구역질나.

☑ No way: 절대 안 돼. 말도 안 돼. 설마

- There's no way you can borrow my toothbrush.
  네가 내 칫솔을 빌릴 일은 절대 없어.

② not to mention

My grandma makes lots of delicious foods for me on my birthday, not to mention 미역국.

우리할머니는 내 생일에 미역국은 말할 것도 없고 많은 맛있는 음식을 나를 위해 만들어주셔.

③ not that I know of

A: Do anchovies have any bad points?
B: No, not that I know of.

A: 멸치에 나쁜 점도 있니?
B: 아니, 내가 알기로는 없는데.

Day 267

① **needless to say**

Needless to say, My mom's cooking is way better than delivery food.

두말할 필요도 없이 우리엄마 음식이 배달음식보다 훨씬 낫지.

② **narrow down**

We had many places that we wanted to go but we finally have narrowed down to two.

우리가 가고 싶은 곳이 많았는데 결국 두 군데로 추려졌어.

☑ narrow: 좁은

③ **not necessarily**

Money doesn't necessarily make you happy.

돈이 꼭 너를 행복하게 해주지는 않아.

☑ not necessarily: 반드시 ~것은 아니다

· A: Does that mean all students have that?
모든 학생들이 다 그것을 가지고 있단 말이니?

B: Not necessarily. 꼭 그렇다는 것은 아니고.

Day 268

① no pain no gain

A: I'm doing push ups to get rid of my pot belly but it's harder than I expected.

B: No pain no gain!

A: 나 뱃살을 빼기위해서 팔굽혀펴기를 하고 있는데 생각보다 힘들어.

B: 고통 없이 얻는 건 없어.

② natural

It's only natural to forget what you've learned. That's why you need to review.

네가 배운 것을 잊어버리는 것은 자연스러운 거야.. 그래서 복습이 필요한 거지.

☑ natural: 자연스러운, 자연의

③ neck and neck

The game was neck and neck.

그 게임은 막상막하였어.

Day 269

① No offense

No offense, but I really thought you were in your 30s.

기분 나쁘게 생각하지 마. 근데 나 정말 네가 30대인 줄 알았어.

☑ No offense: 기분 나쁘게 생각하지 말고 들어주세요.

② nasty

You're being so nasty to your sister.

너 동생한테 너무 못되게 굴고 있어.

☑ nasty: 아주 나쁜, 지독한, 안 좋은

☑ nasty [weather/person/habit …]

· What a nasty smell! 으 고약한 냄새!

③ nearby

Do you think there's a bakery nearby?

가까운 곳에 제과점이 있을까?

☑ nearby [shop/bank …]

Day 270

① notice

A: I got a haircut.

B: Oh! Sorry, I didn't notice.

A: 나 머리 잘랐어.

B: 오! 미안, 몰랐어.

☑ notice: 알아차리다, 눈치를 채다

② nag (at)

I wish my mom would stop nagging (at) me.

엄마가 잔소리 좀 안했으면 좋겠어.

☑ nag: 잔소리하다, 어떤 문제 등으로 걱정하게하다, 불편한 느낌이 들게 들다

☑ nag+sb+[about/to+동사원형]

③ non other than

The owner of the cafe was none other than J K Rolling.

그 카페의 주인은 다름 아닌 제이 케이롤링이었어.

Day 271

① **once**

I get my hair cut once a month.

나는 한 달에 한번 머리를 잘라.

☑ • I have a guitar lesson twice a week. 나는 일주일에 두 번 기타 수업이 있어.

• I brush my teeth three times a day. 나는 하루에 세 번 이를 닦아.

☑ four times / five times …

② **on the weekend**

I usually go to the library on weekends.

나는 주말에는 보통 도서관에 가.

☑ I'm usually busy on weekdays. 나는 주중에는 바빠.

③ **out loud**

Read out loud when you read English!

영어를 읽을 때는 소리를 내어 읽어!

☑ speak out loud / laugh out loud / cry out loud …

Day 272

① **one of**

One of my relatives lives in 울릉도.

우리 친척 중에 한 명이 울릉도에 살아.

☑ two of / some of / most of / all of …

② **on the way**

Could you pick up some milk on the way home?

집에 오는 길에 우유 좀 사다줄래?

☑ on my way / on her way …

③ **on purpose**

I got terrible grades on purpose … not!

나 일부러 아주 나쁜 성적을 받았어 … 뻥이야!

Day 273

① **over there**

Could you put the box over there?

저기에 그 상자를 놓아주시겠어요?

② **on a daily basis**

You should practice English on a daily basis.

너는 매일 영어를 연습해야해.

☑ on a weekly basis / on a monthly basis …

③ **obvious**(=Obviously …)

It is obvious that she isn't interested in her studies.

확실히 그녀는 공부에 흥미가 없어.

☑ obvious: 확실한, 뻔한

Day 274

① one time

One time, I was looking out the window zoning out in class. Suddenly My teacher called on me and I didn't know what to say.

한번은 수업시간에 창밖을 보면서 멍 때리고 있는데 갑자기 선생님이 질문을 하셔서 아무 말도 못했어.

② originally

Originally this place was a factory but people in the village turn it into a cafe.

원래 이곳은 공장이었는데 이곳 사람들이 카페로 개조했어.

☑ · She's(has) always been like that. 그녀는 원래 그래.
· It's(is) supposed to be like this. 이거 원래 이래.

③ of all places

Of all places, why do you want to go to Alaska for your trip?

많은 장소들 중에서 너는 왜 알래스카로 여행을 가고 싶어?

☑ of all people / of all things …

Day 275

① outgoing

He used to be very quiet and shy but now he's very outgoing.

걔는 예전에는 아주 조용하고 부끄러움이 많았었는데 지금은 아주 활발해.

☑ outgoing: 활발한

☑ · He is [introverted/an introvert]. 그는 내성적이야

· He is [extroverted/an extrovert]. 그는 외향적이야

② overwhelm

I was overwhelmed by the size of the place.

나는 그 곳의 크기에 압도당했어.

☑ be overwhelmed [by/with]: (긍정·부정적인) 상황에서 압도당한 느낌이드는

③ open up to

He doesn't open up to others, even to his family.

그는 다른 사람들, 심지어는 가족에게 도 마음을 터놓지 않아.

☑ open up to: ~에게 마음을 열다

Day 276

① **out of nowhere**(=Out of the blue/suddenly)

It was a bright sunny one and out of nowhere there was this heavy rain.

화장한 날씨였는데 느닷없이 폭우가 내렸어.

☑ out of nowhere: 갑자기

② **officially**

Finally, the rainy season has officially started. Stay dry!

드디어 장마가 정식으로 시작되었어. 뽀송뽀송하게 지내!

③ **out of the question**

Viking? I'm not gonna ride that. It's out of the question.

바이킹? 나 그거 안 탈거야. 절대로.

☑ out of the question: 완전 불가능한

Day 277

① **on time**

Please be on time! It starts at exactly two o'clock.

늦지 마!(시간에 맞춰 와)! 정확하게 두 시에 그게 시작할거야.

② **once in a while**

I don't usually eat out but I go to this particular place to enjoy authentic American pizza once in a while.

나는 외식을 잘 안하는데 이따금 정통 미국식 피자를 먹기 위해 그곳을 가곤해.

③ **one-size-fits-all**

A: Do you have this in a bigger size?

B: It's a one-size-fits-all.

A: 더 큰 사이즈 있어요?

B: 그거 프리사이즈예요.

Day 278

① **owe+sb**

I owe you one. Just let me know, if you need a favor.

내가 너한테 신세를 졌다. 너도 부탁할거 있으면 말해~!

☑ I owe you big time. 내가 너한테 신세를 크게 졌다.

② **order out**(=in)

There's nothing to eat. Let's order out!

먹을 게 하나도 없어. 우리 시켜먹자!

☑ order out for pizza: 피자를 시키다

☑ order it out

③ **open**

The store opens at 9 o'clock.

그 가게는 9시에 열어.

☑ The store is open on Sundays as well. 그 가게는 일요일에도 영업을 해.

Day 279

① off the top of one's head

I don't know it off the top of my head.

당장 기억이 안 나네.

☑ off the top of one's head
: 당장 떠오르는 생각으로는, 내 머리에 있는 기억으로는

· A: What's the name of the famous 떡볶이place here?
여기에 유명한 그 떡볶이집 이름이 뭐지?

B: Not off the top of my head. 지금 당장 떠오르지가 않네.

② on and off

I had this stomachache on and off for the past week.

지난 한 주간 이 복통이 생겼다 없어졌다 했어.

☑ on and off: 드문드문, 간간이

· It rained on and off. 비가 왔다 안 왔다 했어.

③ on the fence

I'm on the fence about which club I should join.

나 어떤 동아리에 가입해야 할지 아직 결정 안했어.

☑ on the fence: 이쪽도 저쪽도 아닌

Day 280

① **over and over again**

If you say the word that you find it hard to pronounce over and over again sooner or later, you'll be able to say it naturally.

네가 발음하기 힘든 단어를 계속 반복해서 말하면 곧 그것을 자연스럽게 말할 수 있게 될 거야.

② **once in a blue moon**

I eat fast food once in a blue moon.

내가 패스트푸드를 먹는 것은 극히 드문 일이야.

③ **on top of the world**

I was feeling on top of the world when my book became a bestseller.

내 책이 베스트셀러가 되었을 때 난 기분이 정말 좋았어.

Day 281

① **on the edge of my seat**

The movie was gripping. I was on the edge of my seat throughout the movie.

그 영화는 진짜 재밌었어. 보는 내내 긴장을 늦출 수가 없었어.

② **odds and ends**

We don't use this room. We just keep odds and ends here.

우리는 이 방을 안 써. 여기에는 그냥 잡동사니를 보관해.

③ **on second thought**(=have second thoughts)

On second thought, may be having this annual get-together isn't a good idea.

다시 생각해보니까, 이 연례모임을 갖는 것은 좋은 생각이 아닌 것 같아.

☑ 생각, 결정을 바꿀 때

☑ without a second thought: 곧바로, 즉시

Day 282

① **over the top**

Look at my outfit! Is it over the top?

내 옷 좀 봐봐! 너무 오버인가?

② **on a scale of**

But the one that I tried the other day was … on a scale of 1 to 10, it was a 9.

그런데 얼마 전에 먹어본 것은 1부터 10까지 등급을 매긴다면 9야.

③ **own up**

Own up! I know you ate my sandwich.

자백해! 네가 내 샌드위치 먹은 거 알고 있거든.

☑ own up: 잘못한 것을 인정하다, 고백하다

- own up to stealing the money
- own up to what you've done
- own up to your mistake

Day 283

① plan

I'm planning to read one book a week.

나는 일주일에 책 한권씩을 읽을 계획이야.

= I'm planning on reading …

② point out

Could you point out my mistakes when I speak English?

내가 영어로 말할 때 내 실수들을 지적해주시겠어요?

☑ point out: 지적하다, 가리키다

③ pack

A: Have you finished packing yet?
B: Yes… Oh, I forgot to pack my swimming suit.

A: 짐은 다 쌌니?
B: 응… 아, 내 수영복 싸는 것을 깜박했네.

☑ pack: 짐, 가방을 싸다 / 묶음

Day 284

① put on

The floor is cold. I'll put on my socks.

바닥이 차가워. 양말 신어야지.

☑ put on: 입다/신다/쓰다/끼다 …

☑ Let me put the backpack on. 그 가방 내가 맬게.

↔ take off

② promise

I promise I won't do it again.

약속해 다시는 안 그럴게.

☑ promise+[to+동사원형 / (that)주어+동사]

I promise myself+[to+동사원형 / (that)주어+동사]

③ prefer

A: Which do you prefer, January or December?

B: I prefer December to January.

A: 너는 어느 것이 더 좋니, 1월 아니면 12월?

B: 나는 일월보다 12월이 더 좋아.

☑ prefer to eat = prefer eating

Day 285

① particular

Do you have any particular reason why you don't like dogs?

네가 개를 싫어하는 특별한 이유라도 있니?

☑ particular: 특정한 / 사람이 까다로운

· I wasn't particularly interested in going there but my friend insisted.
  나는 특별히 거기에 가는데 관심이 없었지만 내 친구가 가자고해서.

② pull st off

I don't think I can pull it off.

(그 옷) 내가 소화할 수 없을 것 같은데.

☑ pull+st+off: 훌륭히 해내다

③ put up with

I can't put up with this hot weather any longer.

나 이 더운 날씨를 더 이상 견딜 수가 없어.

☑ put up with: 참다, 견디다

Day 286

① **prepare**

I prepared something for my grandpa's birthday.

내가 우리 할아버지 생신을 위해서 뭔가를 준비했어.

☑ prepare a test: 시험문제를 직접 만들다

prepare for a test: 시험에 대비하다

② **put lotion on**

A: My hands are so dry.

B: Why don't you put some lotion on your hands?

A: 손이 너무 건조해.

B: 손에 로션 좀 바르지 그러니?

☑ 스킨: toner

③ **pouring**

A: Is it raining?

B: It's pouring.

A: 비 오니?

B: 비가 엄청 많이 오고 있어.

Day 287

① **put off**(=postpone)

Try not to put things off unless it's absolutely necessary. It'll become a habit.

정말 필요할 때가 아니라면 할 일을 미루지 마. 그게 습관이 될 테니.

☑ put off: 미루다, 연기하다

② **play safe**

To play safe, I'm going to go the way I know or else I might get lost.

안전하게 내가 아는 길로 갈 거야 그렇지 않으면 길을 잃을 수도 있어.

③ **properly**

Did you read the instructions properly?

너 설명서 제대로 읽었니?

Day 288

① pester for

My niece kept pestering me for candy and I gave in.

우리 조카가 사탕 사달라고 계속 졸라대서 결국 내가 졌지.

☑ pester for: ~조르다, 졸라대다

☑ pester+sb+to / pester+sb+for

② pig out on

I pigged out on popcorn while watching the movie.

영화 보는 동안 팝콘을 엄청 먹었어.

③ put sb through

Do you think your parents put you through this?

너의 부모님 때문에 네가 이것을 겪고있다고 생각하니?

☑ put+sb+through: 나쁜, 어려운 상황을 겪게 하다, 경험하게 하다

Day 289

① **peel off**

Peel off the skins and cut the potatoes into small cubes.

감자껍질을 벗기고 작은 큐브모양으로 썰어.

② **pet peeves**

A: What are your pet peeves?

B: I hate it when people throw their trash away on the street.

A: 너를 짜증나게 하는 게 뭐니?

B: 나는 사람들이 길거리에 쓰레기를 버리는 게 너무 싫어.

③ **pull in**

We can pull in there. The car is pulling out.

우리 저기에 차 세우자. 저 차 나간다.

☑ pull over: 차를 갓길에 세우다

Day 290

① **pile up**

The dishes are piling up. I think I need to do the dishes first.

그릇이 쌓이고 있어. 먼저 설거지부터 해야 할 것 같아.

☑ pile up: 쌓다, 쌓이다

experiences pile up: 경험이 쌓이다

② **personally**

Personally, I prefer hot food to cold food.

개인적으로, 난 찬 음식보다는 따뜻한 음식을 더 좋아해.

☑ Don't take it personally!
너를 겨냥해서 한 말이 아니야. (너를 비난했다고 생각하지 마)

③ **put up**

Is it okay to put up this poster on this wall?

이 벽에 이 포스터를 붙여도 될까?

☑ put up: 붙이다

☑ put+sb+down: 내려놓다 / 비난하다, 모욕하다

· Put it down on the floor! 그거 바닥에 내려놔!

Day 291

① pass out

I almost passed out when I saw the cockroach.

내가 바퀴벌레를 봤을 때 기절할 뻔했어.

☑ pass out: 기절하다, 나눠주다

☑ pass out flyers: 전단지를 나눠주다

② pick

Have you ever picked fruit? By the way don't pick your nose.

너 과일 따 본 적 있니? 그나저나 코 좀 파지마.

☑ There are so many choices. I can't just pick (out) one.
선택권이 너무 많아. 나 하나만 못 고르겠어.

③ pay back

A: Can you lend me 10,000 won?

B: Are you going to pay me back?

A: 나 만원만 빌려주라.

B: 너 갚을 거야?

☑ pay back: 돈을 갚다 / 복수하다

Day 292

① pick up

I'm going to pick up some groceries on the way home.

나 집에 가는 길에 식료품 살 거야.

☑ pick up: 줍다 / 사다 / 데리러가다 / 대화하다 …

- My dad is going to pick me up at the airport.
  우리아빠가 공항으로 나를 데리러 오실거야.

② pay attention to

You should pay attention to what you eat.

네가 먹는 것에 주의를 기울여야 해.

③ pop up

These little banners keep popping up on the screen.

이 조그만 광고들이 화면에 계속 떠.

☑ pop up: 갑자기 나타나다

☑ pop-up cards

Day 293

① pan out

As I've just started to read, I don't know how this story is going to pan out.

이제 막 읽기 시작해서 이야기가 어떻게 전개될지는 모르겠어.

☑ pan out: 이야기 · 상황 등이 전개되다, 펼쳐지다

② put st away

Can you put them away? We're gonna have dinner soon.

그것들 좀 치워줄래? 우리 곧 저녁 먹을 거야.

☑ put st away: 제자리로 갖다놓다

③ play a role in

My best friend played a big role in how I met my master.

우리 사부님을 만나는 데에는 나의 가장 친한 친구가 큰 역할을 했지.

Day 294

① **pass away**

My grandpa passed away when I was five years old.

우리 할아버지는 내가 다섯 살 때 돌아가셨어.

② **pay for**

Did you pay for the meal? I didn't.

너 밥값 냈니? 나는 안냈는데.

☑ pay for: 돈을 지불하다 / 행동이나 일에 대해 대가를 지불하다

- You've got to pay for what you did.
  네가 한 행동에 대해 대가를 지불해야 해.

☑ pay+sb+[to/for]

- pay some money

③ **put sb on the spot**

Don't put her on the spot by asking if she had a nose job. She did it.

그녀한테 코 수술 했냐고 질문해서 난처하게 하지 마. 진짜 했으니까.

☑ put+sb+on the spot
: (답하기 어려운 질문으로) 난처하게 하다, 곤란하게하다

Day 295

① **put out**

luckily, the fire fighters were abe to put out the fire before it got bigger.

다행히도 소방관들이 그 불이 더 커지기전에 끌 수 있었어.

☑ put out: 불을 끄다, 진압하다

② **protect A from B**

People use sunscreen to protect their skin from the sun.

사람들은 햇빛으로부터 피부를 보호하기위해 썬크림을 사용해.

☑ protect A from B: A를 B로부터 보호하다

③ **play devil's advocate**

I'm just playing devil's advocate to make this conversation more interesting.

나는 대화를 좀 더 재미있게 만들기 위해서 일부러 반대 입장에 서있는 거야.

Day 296

① **remember**

Do you remember the store where we bought some cards the other day?

우리가 며칠 전에 카드를 몇 개 샀던 그 가게를 기억하니?

☑ remember: 기억하다

☑ remember ing -했던 것을 기억하다

remember to -할 것을 기억하다

② **run into**(=bump into)

I ran into 칠득 at the mall today.

나 오늘 쇼핑몰에서 칠득이를 우연히 만났어.

③ **recommend**

I recommend this dish. It's really good.

나는 이 음식을 추천해. 이거 정말 맛있어.

☑ recommend [명사/동사ing/that+주어+동사]

Day 297

① regret

I regret eating too many cookies.

쿠키를 너무 많이 먹은 게 후회돼.

☑ regret+(that)주어+동사

regret not+동사ing

② root for

A: Which team are you rooting for?

B: Of course, I'm rooting for the Korean team.

A: 너는 어느 팀을 응원하니?

B: 물론 나는 우리 한국 팀을 응원하지.

③ replace A with B

Do you think many companies will replace their workers with robots?

너는 많은 회사들이 그들의 직원들을 로봇으로 대체할 거라고 생각하니?

☑ replace A with B: A를 B로 바꾸다, 대체하다

Day 298

① **ruin**(=blow/screw up)

The rain ruined my camping.

그 비가 내 캠핑을 망쳤어.

② **remind sb of**

This flower always reminds me of my childhood. My sister and I used to call this flower 계란꽃.

이 꽃은 항상 나의 어린 시절을 떠올리게 해. 내동생과 나는 이 꽃을 계란 꽃이라고 부르곤 했어.

☑ Please, remind me to buy some batteries. 나 배터리 사라고 말 좀 해줘.

③ **roughly**

Roughly chop the cucumber!

오이를 대충(막) 썰어!

☑ roughly: 대략, 대충, 거칠게

· There were roughly 20 people. 대략 20명 정도가 있었어.

Day 299

① reassure

It's reassuring that we have someone who knows the place inside out.

우리 중에 거기를 잘 아는 사람이 있어서 안심이야.

☑ reassure: 안심시키다

· I was reassured to … 안심이 되다

· He reassured me that … 안심시키다

② recently

I recently saw a movie that I watched a long time ago.

나 최근에 오래전에 봤던 영화를 봤어.

③ rest assured

Please, rest assured! I know that area like the back of my hand.

안심해! 나 그 지역 완전 잘 알아.

Day 300

① **regardless of**

People will love this food, regardless of where they're from.

그들이 어디에서 왔든 사람들은 이 음식을 좋아할 거야.

☑ regardless of: ~와 관계없이

② **religiously**

I make the bed religiously every morning because I heard many successful people do it.

나는 매일 아침 침대정리를 어김없이 해 왜냐하면 많은 성공한 사람들이 그렇게 한대.

☑ religiously: 규칙적으로, 꾸준히

③ **right away**

Do it right away!Don't put it off!

지금 당장 해!미루지 말고!

Day 301

① run out

This pen ran out. I got it only a couple of months ago.

이 볼펜 다 썼네. 두세 달 전에 샀는데.

☑ We've run out of toilet paper.

② roll up

Roll up the mat after using it!

매트를 사용한 후에는 감아놔!

☑ roll up: 돌돌 감다

↔ spread out 넓게 펴다

③ rule out

I was ruled out for the game because I had a leg cast.

나는 다리에 깁스를 해서 그 게임에서 제외 되었어.

☑ rule out: 제외하다, 배제하다

Day 302

① **run away**

Don't run away from the dog. Just stay there.

그 개한테서 도망가지 마! 그냥 거기에 서있어.

☑ run away: 도망가다, 피하다

② **rather**

It's rather hard. I thought it would be easy since it's for elementary school students.

이거 생각보다 꽤 어려운데. 난 이게 초등학생들을 위한 거라 쉬울 거라 생각했거든.

③ **run an errand**(=do an errand)

I'm going out to run some errands. I won't be long.

나 볼일 좀 보러 나가. 금방 올 거야.

☑ run an errand: 심부름하다 / 볼일을 보다(은행, 우체국, 쇼핑 등)

Day 303

① rush

There's no need to rush.

서두를 필요 없어.

☑ rush: 서두르다/빠르게 움직이다

· I'm in a rush

☑ rushed [to/into/out of/through …]

② rub it in

A: When was the last time you did plank? You haven't done it in ages.

B: I know, you don't have to rub it in.

A: 너 마지막으로 플랭크 한 게 언제니? 너 안한지 진짜 오래됐지.

B: 나도 알고 있거든. 그만 말해

☑ rub it in: 들먹이다

③ rusty

My English is kind of rusty. I need to brush up on it.

내 영어실력이 좀 녹슬었어. 연습이 필요해.

Day 304

① run of the mill

It was just a run of the mill story. But may be that's why it could appeal to people who'd had enough of Hollywood blockbuster movies.

그건 지극히 평범한 스토리야. 어쩌면 그게 할리우드 블록버스터에 식상한 사람들에게 어필할 수 있었던 이유일지도 모르지.

② rip off

That's a rip off. You shouldn't have bought anything at the tourist spot.

그거 바가지야. 너는 관광지에서 어떤 것도 사지 말았어야해.

☑ I've been ripped off. 바가지 썼어.

③ ride out

I know it's freezing cold. But if we ride out this cold winter, we'll soon have warm spring.

맞아, 정말 추워. 하지만 이 추운 겨울을 이겨내면 곧 따뜻한 봄이 올 거야.

☑ ride out: 이겨내다, 견뎌내다

Day 305

① **say**

A: What did he say to you?(=What did he say?)

B: He said he wanted to eat 붕어빵.

A: 그가 너한테 뭐라고 말했어?

B: 그가 붕어빵 먹고 싶다고 말했어.

☑ say: 말하다

· Say '안녕하세요' when you greet someone.
누군가에게 인사를 할 때는 '안녕하세요'라고 말해!

② **speak**

Do you speak any foreign language besides English?

너 영어 말고 다른 외국어 하는 거 있니?

☑ speak: 말하다

· Did you speak with the manager? 너 매니저하고 얘기했니?
= Did you talk with the manager?

③ **say hello to+sb**

Please say hello to your sister!

언니한테 안부 전해줘!

Day 306

① **still**

I had some snacks but I'm still hungry.

나 간식을 좀 먹었는데 그래도(아직도) 배고파.

② **stir**

Stir your 미숫가루 before you drink!

마시기전에 미숫가루를 저어!

③ **sticky**

I spilt some honey on the table so it's kind of sticky.

내가 식탁에 꿀을 쏟아서 조금 끈적끈적해.

Day 307

① **slow down**

slow down! There's a speed bump.

속도 줄여! 과속 방지턱이 있어.

② **such as**

I like winter snacks such as 호떡 and 붕어빵.

나는 겨울간식들을 좋아해 호떡이나 붕어빵 같은

☑ such as: 예를 들면

☑ such as + 명사

for example + (회화에서는) 명사, 구, 절 다 올 수 있음.

③ **start to**(=start ~ing)

We were in the park and suddenly It started to rain.

우리는 공원에 있었는데 갑자기 비가 오기 시작했어.

Day 308

① **stay**

I'm going to just stay (at) home this weekend.

나는 이번 주말에 그냥 집에 있을 거야.

☑ stay: ~에 있다, 머물다

☑ Stay [healthy/happy/cool/dry …]

It's freezing cold. Stay warm! 정말 추워. 따뜻하게 지내!

② **steep**

Wow, the elevator is really long and steep. I feel dizzy.

와, 엘리베이터가 진짜 길고 경사가 심하다. 나 어지러워.

☑ steep: 경사진, 비싼, (물 등에) 담그다 우리다

stiff: 딱딱한, 결리는, 경직된 / 비싼

☑ steep, stiff: 가격이 매우 비싼

steep(stiff) [price/fee/penalty …]

③ **set st/sb apart**

Using only one color for his paintings sets his pictures apart from others.

그의 그림이 다른 것들과 달라 보이는 것은 그림에 단 한 가지 색만을 사용해서야.

Day 309

① **shop around**

It's exhausting to shop around to get what I want even on the internet.

원하는 것을 사기위해 상점들을 돌아다니는 것은 정말 피곤해 인터넷도 마찬가지고.

② **sign up for**

I signed up for an English course last year but I attended only twice.

나 작년에 영어수업에 등록했었는데 두 번밖에 출석을 안했어.

☑ sign up for: 가입하다, 등록하다, 신청하다 / 하기로 하다

- I didn't sign up for this. 나 이거 한다고 한적 없어.

③ **settle down**

Okay, everybody, settle down. let's watch the movie.

자, 여러분, 조용히 하고. 영화 봅시다.

☑ settle down: 정착하다, 진정하다, 조용히 하다

Day 310

① so 형용사/부사 that 주어 동사

I was so exhausted that I couldn't even walk.

나 너무 피곤해서 걸을 수도 없었어.

☑ so ~ that: 너무 ~해서~하다

☑ Read more so that you can be smarter.
네가 더 똑똑해질 수 있도록 책들을 더 읽어.

· so that: ~할 수 있도록

② spend

I usually spend my free time walking in the park.

나는 보통 공원을 걸으면서 자유시간을 보내.

☑ spend: 돈을 쓰다 / 시간을 보내다

☑ spend on+명사 / spend+동사ing

· I spend my allowance on school supplies. 나는 내 용돈을 학용품 사는데 써.

③ speaking of(=speaking of which)

Speaking of christmas, do you have any best or the worst memory of christmas?

크리스마스 얘기가 나와서 말인데 너는 가장 좋았던 혹은 아주 안 좋았던 크리스마스 기억이 있니?

Day 311

① slightly

It's slightly different from this one.

이것은 이것과 약간 다른데.

② show off

Did you get this because you needed or to show off?

너 이거 필요해서 산거야 아니면 자랑하려고 산거야?

☑ show off: 자랑하다

- He is such a show-off. 그는 늘 잘난 척이야.

③ It's a shame

It was a real shame that we could stay there only two days.

거기에서 이틀밖에 머물지 못해 정말 아쉬웠어.

☑ It's a shame: 아쉬운, 안타까운, 유감스러운

☑ It's a shame [that+주어+동사 / to+동사원형 / about+명사]

☑ What a shame!

Day 312

① **something comes up.**

I was going to call you yesterday but something came up.

어제 너한테 전화하려고 했는데 일이 좀 생겼어.

② **seem**

A: 칠득 seemed tired last week.

B: Yeah, he seems to have some problems at work.

A: 칠득이 지난주에 피곤해보이더라.

B: 응, 직장에서 문제가 좀 있는 것 같아.

☑ seem: ~해 보이다

- It seems like it's going to rain. 비 올 것 같아. (= It looks like......)

③ **suggest**

My dad suggested going to 부산 instead of 제주도.

우리 아빠가 제주도 대신 부산에 가자고 제안했어.

☑ suggest+[명사/that 주어+동사/w의문사]

Day 313

① **specifically**(=in detail)

Please, tell me specifically!

구체적으로 말해주세요!

② **send**(=send+st+to+sb)

My grandma sent us sweet potatoes that she grew herself.

우리 할머니가 직접 기르신 고구마를 우리에게 보내주셨어.

③ **suffer from**

I suffer from a pollen allergy every spring.

봄마다 알레르기 때문에 고생을 해.

Day 314

① **sweat**

It's only April but I'm sweating already.

4월밖에 안됐는데 나 벌써 땀나.

☑ I sweat a lot. 나는 땀이 많이 나.

② **several**

I have several ideas. Pick one that you like the most.

나한테 몇 가지의 아이디어가 있어. 네가 가장 마음에 드는 걸로 하나 골라.

③ **stay up late**

I like weekends because I can stay up late.

난 주말이 좋아 늦게까지 안 자도 되니까.

= stay up late. 늦게까지 깨어있다

☑ stay out late: 늦게까지 밖에서 시간을 보내다

Day 315

① **sooner or later**

Sooner or later, leaves will turn red, orange, yellow and fall off from trees.

곧 나뭇잎들이 빨간색, 오렌지색, 노란색으로 변할 거고 나무들에서 떨어질 거야.

② **set aside**(=put aside)

You've got to set aside some time for your English studies on a daily basis or else it's so hard to make English a part of your life.

매일 영어 공부할 시간을 따로 떼어놔야지 그렇지 않으면 영어를 너의 생활의 일부로 만드는 것은 정말 힘들어.

☑ set aside: 시간, 돈 등을 따로 두다

③ **spill**

I spilt water all over my laptop.

나 노트북에 물을 쏟았어.

☑ spill - spilled(spilt)

Day 316

① **step in**

Don't step in the argument between them. You'll just waste your breath.

그들의 논쟁에 끼어들지 마! 그냥 헛수고만 하는 거니까.

☑ step in: 끼어들다, 간섭하다

② **splatter**

The oil splattered all over the place when I placed the tofu in the pan.

내가 두부를 후라이팬에 넣을 때 기름이 여기저기 다 튀었어.

③ **strain**

You're looking at your cell phone too long. Don't strain your eyes!

너 너무 오랫동안 핸드폰 본다. 눈을 혹사시키지 마!

☑ strain: 무리하다

· strain a muscle

= put a strain on+st

Day 317

① **slowly but surly**

If you do this exercise on a daily basis, slowly but surly it'll build strength in your entire body.

네가 만약에 이 운동을 매일하면 느리지만 확실히 너의 몸 전체의 힘을 길러줄 거야.

② **shy away from**

Don't shy away from making mistakes when it comes to speaking English.

영어를 할 때 실수하는 것을 피하지 마.

☑ shy away from: 뭔가 두려운 감정이 있어서 피하다

③ **search for**

I tried to search for the information about it online but I couldn't.

내가 온라인에서 그 정보를 찾으려고 했는데 못 찾았어.

☑ search for: ~을 찾다, 조사하다

Day 318

① **suit**

You've got to find your own way to study English that suits you the most.

너는 영어공부를 하기위해 너에게 가장 잘 맞는 방법을 찾아야해.

② **somewhere along the line**

Somewhere along the line that place became one of the popular spots among tourists.

언제부터인가 거기가 관광객들 사이에서 인기 있는 곳 중에 한 곳이 되었어.

③ **sought after**

He's the most sought after expert in stock markets lately.

그는 요즘에 가장 잘 나가는 주식시장 전문가야.

Day 319

① **sort out**

It's a hassle to sort out the trash but it's crucial for the environment.

쓰레기를 분류하는 것은 번거로운 일이지만 환경을 위해 매우 중요해.

☑ sort out: 분류하다, 정리하다, 해결하다

- Don't worry! I'll sort that out. 걱정 마! 내가 해결할게.

② **see off**

Are you going to see off your friend at the airport?

너 친구 배웅하러 공항에 갈거니?

☑ see off: 배웅하다(굿바이 하러 공항이나 역으로 가다)

☑ I'll walk you out to the door. 문까지 배웅해 드릴게요.

↔ 마중하다: pick+sb+up / pick up+sb / meet+sb

③ **stand up for**

You should learn to stand up for yourself!

너는 너 자신을 위해 맞설 수 있어야해.

☑ stand up for+[sb/st]: ~을 옹호하다, 변호하다 / ~의 편이 되다

Day 320

① stand for

A: What does LOL stand for?

B: It stands for laughing out loud.

A: LOL은 무슨 뜻이야?

B: 그것은 'laughing out loud'크게 웃다란 의미야.

☑ stand for: ~를 지지하다

② surround

The place is surrounded by high buildings.

그곳은 고층건물들로 둘러싸여있어.

③ show up

We were to meet there at two but she didn't show up on time as usual.

우리가 거기서 두시에 만나기로 했는데 그녀는 여느 때처럼 제시간에 나타나지 않았어.

☑ show up: (보통 늦게 혹은 기대하지 않았을 때) 약속 장소에 나타나다 / 뭔가가 보이다, 나타나다

Day 321

① stay away from

I should stay away from sweets and greasy food.

나는 단것이랑 기름진 음식을 피해야해.

☑ stay away from: 멀리하다, 피하다

stay away from+[st/sb]

② spice up

The sesame oil will spice up the dish.

그 참기름이 그 요리의 맛을 더해줄 거야.

☑ spice up: 맛, 재미, 흥미 등을 더하다

spice up [a story/a place …]

③ self-conscious

I was a bit self-conscious as I was the only Asian there.

거기에 아시아인이 나 혼자였기 때문에 조금 남들이 의식이 되더라고.

Day 322

① shake things up

We're going to shake things up and go to a different place to camp.

우리 변화를 좀 주기위해서 다른 곳으로 캠핑을 갈 거야.

☑ shake things up: 쭉 해오던 것과는 다르게 뭔가를 하다

② set up

We should set up the tent first before doing anything else.

우리 다른 거 하기 전에 텐트부터 쳐야 해.

☑ set up: 세우다 / 만들다 / 설정하다 / 마련하다 …

set up [shop/a plan/a system …]

- Why don't we set up an English club ourselves?
  우리가 직접 영어 동아리 만드는 거 어때?

↔ take down a tent

③ stick to

Not many people stick to their new year's resolutions.

새해결심을 지키는 사람은 별로 없어.

☑ stick to: 고수하다

Day 323

① **stand out**

I don't want to stand out wearing this red dress.

나 이 빨간 드레스입고 튀고 싶고 않아.

☑ stand out: 눈에 띄다

② **sleep in**

I'm going to sleep in this weekend. I'm so tired.

난 이번 주말에 푹 잘 거야. 너무 피곤해.

☑ sleep in: 늦게까지 자다

③ **set the alarm**(clock)

I set the alarm for five but it didn't go off.

내가 다섯시로 알람을 맞춰놨는데 울리지 않았어.

☑ set the alarm: 알람을 맞춰놓다

☑ set the [heating/oven/washing machine …]

Day 324

① stop by

Why don't we stop by the convenience store to pick up some water.

물 좀 사게 편의점에 들르자!

② set an example

Before telling your children what to do, try to set an example by doing what you want your kids to do.

너의 아이들에게 무엇을 하라고 시키게 전에 네가 아이들이 했으면 하는 것을 행동으로 보여줘.

☑ set an example: 모범을 보이다

③ Sounds like

Sounds like you're having a blast there.

너 거기서 엄청 신나는 시간을 보내고 있구나.

☑ Sounds like: ~처럼 들리다

· (It) sounds like

Day 325

① **try on**

Can I try this on?

이거 입어 봐도 돼요?

☑ try on: 입어보다

· Why don't you try that on before you buy it?
그거 사기전에 입어보지 그러니?

② **text**

He just texted me back saying he is not able to juin us today.

그가 방금 오늘 우리랑 같이 못 간다고 답 메일 보내왔어.

☑ text = send a message 문자, 메세지를 보내다

③ **take out**(=pull out)

I took out a pen to write down what I heard.

나는 내가 들은 것을 적기위해서 볼펜을 꺼냈어.

Day 326

① team up

We teamed up with B team for the project.

우리는 B팀과 같이 팀을 이뤄 그 프로젝트를 했어.

② the other day

I saw a movie the other day.

나 며칠 전에 영화 봤어.

③ the best ever

The highlight of 추석 was the 갈비찜 that my grandma made. It was the best 갈비찜 ever.

추석에 가장 좋았던건 할머니가 만드신 갈비찜이었어. 내가 먹어본 갈비찜 중에 최고였어.

☑ the best 청국장 ever / the worst movie ever

Day 327

① tell

What did he tell you?

그가 너한테 뭐라고 했어?

= What did he say to you?

☑ tell: 말하다

· Tell me what you saw there! 거기서 뭘 봤는지 말해줘!

② talk

I saw 칠득 talking to someone in front of the convenience store.

나 칠득이가 편의점 앞에서 누군가와 얘기하고 있는 거 봤어.

☑ talk: 말하다

· Let's talk about the countries we want to visit!
우리가 가고 싶은 나라들에 대해서 얘기하자!

☑ talk to = talk with

talk to oneself: 혼잣말하다

③ tell on+sb(=tattle on+sb/snitch on+sb)

Did you tell on me?

네가 나 고자질했니?

☑ tell on+sb: 고자질하다

· I didn't tell mom on you. 엄마한테 널 고자질하지 않았어.

☑ 고자질쟁이: a tattletale, a snitch

Day 328

① **take your time**

Take your time! We still have a plenty of time.

천천히 해! 우리 시간 많아.

② **that**

Is it that hard?

그게 그렇게 힘들어(어려워)?

☑ It's not that important. 그건 그렇게 중요하지 않아.

③ **take care**

A: See you!

B: Take care!

A: 다음에 보자!

B: 다음에 보자!

☑ take care: 조심해(건강, 안전을 당부할 때)

Day 329

① **then**

Then, how about this one?

그러면 이건 어때?

☑ then: 그때는(과거/미래) / 그리고 나서

② **turn on**

Let's turn on the AC! It's boiling hot.

에어컨 켜자! 너무 더워.

↔ turn off 끄다

③ **take a look**

Take a look at this!

이거 봐!

☑ take a look: 자세히 봐! (=Check this out!)

Day 330

① **too ~ to …**

It's too hard to choose only one. I love all of them.

하나만 고르는 건 너무 힘들어. 난 그것들 다 좋아.

☑ too ~ to … : … 하기에 너무 ~하다

② **tend to**

He tends to talk a lot especially when he talks about cooking.

그는 말이 많은 편이야 특히 요리에 대해서 말할 때.

= He has a tendency to …

☑ tend to: 하는 경향이 있다

③ **take a break**

We took a break for half an hour and then we worked again.

우리는 30분 쉬고 난후 다시 일했어.

☑ take a break: 중간에 쉬다

Day 331

① **the thing is**

People know what to do to be a good English speaker but the thing is they don't put it into practice.

사람들은 영어짱이 되려면 뭘 해야 할지 알고 있어 그런데 문제는 실행에 옮기지는 않는다는 거지.

② **the same as**

His situation isn't the same as yours.

그의 상황은 너의 상황하고 달라.

☑ the same as: ~와 같은

③ **take care of**

Don't worry. I'll take care of the rest of it. You go get some rest.

걱정하지 마. 나머지는 내가 할게(처리할게). 너는 가서 쉬어.

☑ take care of: 처리하다, 돌보다

Day 332

① that's why

I'm allergic to nuts. That's why I don't eat peanut butter.

나 견과류 알레르기가 있어. 그래서 땅콩버터 안 먹는 거야.

☑ that's why: 그런 이유로

☑ That's [what/when …]

② the highlight of

A: What was the highlight of the show?

B: To be honest, I fell asleep, so I don't know.

A: 그 쇼에 하이라이트가 뭐였어?

B: 솔직히 말해서, 나 잤어 그래서 몰라.

☑ the highlight of: ~의 가장 좋은 부분

③ thank goodness

Thank goodness you're here. I couldn't have finished it if it weren't for your help.

네가 여기 있어서 다행이야. 너의 도움 없이는 이것을 못 끝냈을 거야.

= It was a good thing

Day 333

① **take turns**

Let's take turns to ask questions! You go first.

우리 돌아가면서 질문을 하자! 너부터 해!

= take turns asking questions …

☑ take turns: 교대로 하다

② **the rest of**

Shall(Should) I put the rest of the pizza in the fridge?

피자 남은 거 냉장고에 넣을까?

= Shall I put the rest in the fridge?

③ **take part in**(=participate in/enter/join)

Do you want to take part in the hot dog eating contest?

너 핫도그 먹기 대회에 참가하고 싶니?

☑ take part in: ~에 참가하다, 참여하다

Day 334

① take sb/st to

My mom took me to the library today.

오늘 우리 엄마가 나를 도서관에 데리고 가셨어.

☑ take ~ to … : ~을(를) …로 데리고 가다 / 가져가다

☑ "to'가 필요없는 단어는 생략
예) take sb(st) there / somewhere / shopping …

② time flies

It's already February. Time flies.

벌써 2월이야. 시간 빠르다.

③ take place

Olympic games take place every four years.

올림픽경기는 4년마다 열려.

= Olympic games are held every four years (*hold - held - held)

☑ take place: 개최하다

Day 335

① **thanks to**

Thanks to my mom, I could do my homework.

엄마 덕분에 숙제를 할 수 있었어.

☑ Thanks to 칠득, we lost the game. 칠득이 덕분에(때문에) 그 게임에서 졌어. (*부정적 의미)

② **take a picture**

I took lots of pictures of spring flowers like cherry blossoms and azaleas.

벚꽃, 진달래 같은 봄꽃 사진을 많이 찍었어.

= take a photo(shot)
get a shot
snap pictures

☑ take selfies: 셀카를 찍다(= take my pictures)

③ **take off**

We can see airplanes taking off from here as well as landing.

우리는 여기서 비행기가 이륙하고 착륙하는 것을 볼 수 있어.

☑ take off: 이륙하다 / 옷을 벗다

Day 336

① throw away

Did you throw away the paper that was on the desk?

책상에 있던 종이 버렸어?

☑ throw away: 버리다

② traditional

윷놀이 is a traditional korean game.

윷놀이는 한국의 전통놀이야.

☑ traditional: 전통적인

③ there is a time

There are times when I don't feel like doing anything.

아무것도 안하고 싶을 때가 있어.

Day 337

① **There's no point in**

There's no point (in) complaining about the weather.

날씨에 대해 불평해봤자 소용없어.

= It's no use complaining about the weather.

② **throughout**

I thought Malaysia is hot throughout the year but it was a bit chilly.

나는 말레이시아는 일 년 내내 더운 줄 알았는데 좀 쌀쌀했어.

☑ throughout the [day/course …]

③ **That's the spirit**

A: No matter how hard it is, I'm gonna make it.
B: That's the spirit!

A: 그게 아무리 힘들어도 나는 꼭 해낼 거야.
B: 바로 그거야!

☑ That's the spirit: 올바른 태도, 정신이다

Day 338

① **turn**

Don't you love autumn leaves? Look! All the leaves turned red, orange and yellow.

가을단풍 너무 좋지 않니? 봐! 모든 나뭇잎들이 빨강, 오렌지, 노란색으로 변했어.

☑ turn 12: 12살이 되다

② **tidy up**

I always tidy up my desk before I study.

나는 항상 공부하기 전에 책상정리부터 해.

☑ tidy up: 정리하다, 깨끗이 하다

③ **turn into**

This robot turns into a car and that's why it's so popular among children.

이 로봇이 자동차로 바뀐다 그래서 이게 아이들 사이에서 인기가 좋은 거야.

☑ turn into: ~로 바뀌다, 변하다

☑ turn into [a bed/a butterfly/a big star …]

Day 339

① the 비교급

The more time you invest in your English the quicker you'll see your progress.

영어공부에 더 많은 시간을 쓸수록 더 빨리 너의 향상을 보게 될 거야.

☑ The 비교급A+주어+동사 (…) the 비교급B 주어+동사
: A 할수록 더 B 하다
The more you study the harder it gets. 공부할수록 더 어려워져.

② take sb/st for granted

You should be grateful for what you have. Don't take anything for granted.

네가 가지고 있는 것에 감사해야해. 그 어느 것도 당연하게 생각하면 안 돼.

☑ take+[sb/st]+for granted: 무엇을/누군가를 당연하게 생각하다

③ take seriously

You tend to take things seriously when you can actually take them lightly.

너는 가볍게 여길 일들도 심각하게 받아들이는 경향이 좀 있더라.

☑ take+[st/sb]+seriously 심각하게 받아들이다
take+[st/sb]+lightly 가볍게 받아들이다

Day 340

① think st over

I thought it over and I decided not to go there.

나 고민을 좀 했는데 거기에 안가기로 했어.

☑ think+st+over / think over+st: 고민하다

② to each his own

A: Some put meat for 된장찌개.

B: I guess, to each his own.

A: 어떤 사람들은 된장찌개에 고기를 넣어.

B: 각각 취향은 다르니까 뭐.

③ take up

I won't take up too much of your time.

네 시간 많이 안 뺏을게.

☑ The sofa takes up too much space. 그 소파가 너무 많은 자리를 차지하는데.

☑ take up a new hobby: 새로운 취미를 가지다

Day 341

① turn out

Actually, I didn't want to go there but it turned out to be one of the best trips ever.

사실 나 거기에 가기 싫었는데 결과적으로는 내가 한 여행 중 최고의 여행 중의 하나가 되었어.

☑ turn out: 생각한 것과 다른 결과가 나오다

- It turns out that he is her brother.
  알고 보니까 그가 그녀의 남동생이더라고.

② tone down

Mom, what's with the red lipstick? I think you should tone it down.

엄마, 그 빨간 립스틱은 뭐야? 좀 연한 색을 바르는 게 낫지 않을까.

☑ tone down: 색, 맛, 말, 글 등의 강도를 낮추다

- tone down the [story/color/speech …]

③ take away

My mom would take away my cell phone if I kept looking at it while having a meal.

만약에 내가 식사하면서 계속 휴대폰을 보면 우리 엄마는 그것을 뺏을 거야.

☑ take away: 뺏어가다

Day 342

① **take a test**

I took a math test today. It wasn't that hard. I have another test tomorrow. I think I'll be okay.

오늘 수학 시험을 봤는데. 그렇게 어렵진 않았어. 내일도 다른 시험이 하나있는데. 뭐 괜찮을 것 같아.

② **tell me about it**

A: Don't you think our new teacher is too strict?

B: Tell me about it!

A: 우리 새로운 선생님 너무 엄격한 것 같지 않니?

B: 내말이! (동의해)

③ **take st apart ↔ put st together/together st**

It was easy to take it apart but it's hard to put it back together again.

그것을 분해하는 것은 쉬웠는데 다시 조립하는 것은 어렵네.

Day 343

① **turn down**(=refuse)

I don't know about you but it's hard for me to turn down when people ask me a favor.

너는 어떨지 모르겠지만 나는 사람들이 나에게 부탁할 때 거절하는 게 힘들어.

☑ turn down: 거절하다

② **take action**

Don't just sit and think! Take action!

그냥 앉아서 생각만하지마! 행동으로 옮겨!

③ **the pros and cons**

What's the pros and cons about having siblings?

형제자매가 있는 것의 장단점이 뭐야?

☑ the pros and cons: 장점과 단점

Day 344

① **take a nap**

I don't normally take a nap but I felt so drowsy after lunch.

나는 보통 낮잠을 안자는데 점심 먹고 난 후에 되게 나른하더라고.

☑ take a nap: 낮잠을 자다

② **take medicine**

Should I go see a doctor or just take medicine?

병원을 갈까 그냥 약을 먹을까?

☑ take medicine: 약을 먹다

☑ take a pill: 알약을 먹다

③ **think of st/sb**

A: I always forget to practice English.

B: Think of it as one of your meals a day.

A: 나는 항상 영어 연습하는 걸 잊어버려.

B: 그것을 하루에 네가 먹는 식사 중에 하나라고 생각해.

Day 345

① **tear away**

It seems like people can't tear themselves away from their cell phones.

사람들이 핸드폰에서 못 떨어지는 것 같아.

☑ tear away: ~을(를)~로부터 떼어놓다, 떨어뜨려놓다

☑ tear / ter / - tore - torn

② **take stairs**

I'll take the stairs not the elevator.

난 엘리베이터가 아니라 계단을 이용할거야.

☑ take stairs: 계단을 이용하다

③ **turn over**

How can I turn over this pancake without a spatular?

뒤집게 없이 이 팬케잌을 어떻게 뒤집지?

☑ turn over: 뒤집다

Day 346

① take a class

I'm going to take a yoga class from next week.

나 다음 주부터 요가 수업 받을 거야.

☑ take a class: 수업을 듣다 (수업을 등록하다의 개념)

☑ have a class(lesson): 이미 등록한 수업을 받는 것

② to a certain degree(=to some degree(extent))

I guess he's right to a certain degree.

그의 말이 어느 정도는 맞다고 생각해.

③ take a trip(=go on a trip)

If you could take a trip now where would you like to go?

만약에 네가 지금 여행을 갈 수 있다면 어디를 가고 싶니?

☑ take a trip: 여행을 가다

Day 347

① **tap into**

You can write a great story by tapping into your own experiences as well as creativity.

너의 창의력과 너 자신의 경험들을 이용해서 훌륭한 스토리를 쓸 수 있어.

☑ tap into: 활용하다, 이용하다 / 다가가다(접근하다)

② **that's news to sb**(=That's unheard of)

Over 20 years old? Wow, that's news to me. I thought they could buy alcohol when they're 16 years old.

20살이 넘어야 한다고? 그건 몰랐네. 나는 그들은 16살이면 술을 살수 있다고 생각했거든.

☑ that's news to sb: 금시초문이다

③ **transfer**

We need to transfer once to get there.

우리 거기 가려면 한번 갈아타야해.

☑ transfer: 사람, 장소, 교통수단, 지위 등으로부터 다른 것으로 옮기다

transfer to line number 2 2호선으로 갈아타다

transfer to another school 전학가다, 편입하다

Day 348

① **take the liberty**

I took the liberty of ordering the food. I hope you don't mind.

음식 내 맘대로 시켰어. 기분 안 상하길.

② **tie**

Tie it tightly so that it won't come undone.

안 풀리게 꽉 묶어.

☑ tie: 묶다 / 비기다

☑ It's a tie. / We tied. 비겼어.

③ **talk sb into**(=win sb over)

I was able to talk my parents into going to an amusement park.

나는 우리 부모님을 놀이공원에 가자고 설득할 수 있었어.

☑ talk sb into: ~하도록 설득하다

↔ talk sb out of st ~하지 않도록 설득하다

Day 349

① **throw a party**(=have a party)

He is going to throw a party this Friday.

그가 이번 금요일에 파티를 열거야.

☑ throw a party: 파티를 열다

② **take it back**

A: You're the shortest one in your class, aren't you?

B: No! Take it back!

A: 네가 반에서 키가 제일 작지, 그치?

B: 아니거든. 그 말 취소해!

③ **too good to be true**

I thought it was a scam because it was too good to be true.

난 그게 너무 완벽하게 좋아서 사기인줄 알았어.

☑ too good to be true: 너무 좋아서 믿어지지 않는

Day 350

① **used to**

He used to eat lots of junk food but not any longer.

그는 예전에는 불량식품을 많이 먹곤 했지만 지금은 아니야.

☑ used to: 예전에 ~하곤 하다

☑ [be/get] used to+동사ing ~에 익숙해지다

② **undercooked**

I like my ramen a bit undercooked. What about you?

나는 라면이 꼬들꼬들한 게 좋아. 넌 어때?

☑ undercooked: 덜 익은

overcooked: 너무 익은

soggy: 면이 불은

③ **up one's alley**

That's right up my alley. As a hair stylist, I'll tell you what you should do.

그건 내가 전문이지(나의 관심분야). 헤어스타일리스트로서 네가 뭐해야 하는지 알려줄게.

Day 351

① **unlike**

Unlike his brother, he is very quiet and reserved.

그의 형과는 달리, 그는 굉장히 조용하고 내성적이야.

② **up in the air**

Our plan to go to South Africa is up in the air.

남아프리카로의 여행은 아직 미정이야.

☑ up in the air: 계획 등이 불확실한

③ **under the weather**

I feel under the weather today. I'll just stay home.

나 오늘 몸이 안 좋아. 그냥 집에 있을래.

☑ out of sorts: 몸 혹은 기분이 좀 안 좋을 때

Day 352

① **up to**

A: Where should we go for dinner?

B: It's up to you. I'm up for anything.

A: 우리 저녁 먹으러 어디에 갈까?

B: 너 맘대로 해. 난 아무거나 괜찮아.

☑ up to: ~에 달려있는 / (숫자,수준 정도가) 최대~까지 / (시간)~까지 / ~할 능력이 있는 / 꿍꿍이가 있는

② **under control**

Don't worry! Everything is under control.

걱정하지 마! 모든 것이 잘 진행되고 있어.

③ **used up**

I've used up all the flour making pancakes.

나 팬 케잌 만드느라 밀가루 다 썼어.

Day 353

① **wake up**

I woke up at seven but didn't get up till seven ten.

나 일곱 시에 깼는데 7시10분까지 안 일어났어.

☑ wake up: 잠에서 깨다

② **worry about**(=I'm worried)

I don't worry about my future because I believe if I do my best every day, I'll have a good future.

나는 나의 미래에 대해서 걱정하지 않아 왜냐하면 내가 매일 최선을 다해 살면 나의 미래가 좋을 것을 믿거든.

☑ worry about: ~에 대해 걱정하다

③ **written all over your face**

A: I'm so excited to go to 제주도 this weekend.

B:I know. Its written all over your face.

A: 이번 주에 제주도에 가서 정말 신나.

B: 알아. 너 얼굴에 다 쓰여 있어.

☑ = I can tell ((that) you're happy).

Day 354

① **watch out**(=Be careful!/look out!)

Watch out! A car is coming.

조심해! 차가 오고 있어.

☑ Watch out for cars!

② **work out**

Our plan didn't work out.

우리 계획은 성공적으로 이루어지지 않았어.

☑ work out: 성공적으로 이루어지다

☑ Do you work out at the gym? 너는 헬스클럽에서 운동하니?

③ **What a waste**

You're going to throw away all the foods? What a waste!

너 그 음식들을 다 버리려고? 아깝다!

☑ What a waste: 아깝다, 헛수고다

☑ a waste of time: 시간낭비

a waste of money: 돈낭비

a waste of one's talents: 재능낭비

· Don't waste your time! 시간낭비하지 마!

Day 355

① wait for

A: Are you waiting for something or someone?

B: I'm waiting to see if more people are coming.

A: 너 뭔가 아니면 누군가를 기다리고 있는 중이니?

B: 사람들이 더 오는지 보려고 기다리는 중이야.

② What seems to be the problem?

A: What seems to be the problem?

B: I have a fever, a runny nose….

A: 어디가 아프세요?

B: 저 열도 있고 콧물도 나오고….

☑ What seems to be the problem?: 뭐가(어디에) 문제가 있나요?

② win the lottery

If you won the lottery what would you do with the money?

네가 만약에 복권에 당첨이 되면 뭘 할 거야?

☑ win the lottery: 복권에 당첨이 되다

Day 356

① **want sb/st to**

I want my family to be happy and healthy.

나는 우리 가족이 행복하고 건강했으면 좋겠어.

☑ want sb/st to 동사원형: 누군가 혹은 무엇이 어떻기를 원하다

- I want to eat something sweet. 나 뭔가 단 게 먹고 싶어.
- I want+명사

② **what else**

A: Swimsuit, swim cap, goggles, snorkel… what else do I need?
B: Floaties? (a floaty)

A: 수영복, 수영모자, 수경, 스노클… 뭐가 또 필요하지?
B: 튜브?

☑ what else: 또 다른 것은? (=anything else?)

③ **warm up**

Cold pizza or should I warm it up?

식은 피자 그냥 먹을래 아니면 덥힐까?

☑ warm up: 따뜻하게 하다 / 준비운동을 하다

☑ Let's warm up before the game. 게임하기 전에 준비운동하자!

Day 357

① **with the naked eye**

It's microscopic. You can hardly see it with the naked eye.

그건 정말 조그매. 육안으로는 보기 힘들어.

② **would rather A than B**

I would rather stay at home than go shopping.

나는 쇼핑을 가느니 차라리 집에 있을래.

☑ would rather A than B: B 하느니 차라리 A 하겠다

③ **wing it**(=play it by ear)

A: Have you prepared the presentation?

B: No, I'm just going to wing it.

A: 너 발표 준비는 했니?

B: 아니, 그냥 즉석에서 하려고.

☑ wing it: 사전 준비, 계획 없이 즉흥적으로 하다

Day 358

① wonder

I wonder why she looks so down today.

그녀가 왜 그렇게 오늘 시무룩한지 궁금하네.

☑ You pulled an all-nighter? No wonder you look tired.
밤 샜다고? 네가 피곤해 보이는 것도 당연하네.

② when it comes to

Repetition is paramount when it comes to learning English.

영어를 배우는 데에 있어서 반복은 정말 중요해.

☑ when it comes to+[명사/동사ing]: ~에 있어서는/~에 대해서는

③ What's wrong with

What's wrong with your hair?

너 머리가 왜 그래?

= What happened to your hair?

Day 359

① -wise(=in terms of)

A: How was the restaurant you went for dinner yesterday?

B : It was a bit expensive price-wise but food-wise it was excellent.

A: 어제 저녁 식사하러 갔던 식당 어땠어?

B: 가격 면에서는 조금 비쌌지만 음식은(음식 면에서는) 완전 맛있었어.

☑ -wise: ~면에서는

- career-wise / weather-wise / money-wise …

② what comes to mind when you think of st/sb?

A: What comes to mind when you think of winter?

B: Christmas, Santa, snow, vacation, roasted sweet potatoes and of course 붕어빵.

A: 겨울하면 뭐가 떠오르니?

B: 크리스마스, 산타, 눈, 방학, 군고구마 그리고 물론 붕어빵.

③ What+형용사+명사(주어+동사)

Check it out! What a tall building!

저것 봐! 정말 높은 빌딩이다!

☑ what: (감탄할 때) ~구나!

☑ How+[형용사/부사] (주어+동사)

- How tall (the building is)!
- What a tall building (it is)!

Day 360

① when you grow up

칠득, when you grow up, what do you want to do?

칠득아, 너는 이다음에 크면 뭘 하고 싶니?

② What do you like about

What do you like about summer break?

넌 여름방학의 어떤 점이 좋니?

↔ What do you not like about ...?

③ wait in line

Though it was a week day, I had to wait in long lines to go on some of the popular rides.

주중이었지만 인기 있는 것들을 타기위해서는 긴 줄에서 기다려야만 했어.

☑ wait in line: 줄에 서서 기다리다

☑ stand in line: 줄을 서다

Day 361

① whatsoever

He did nothing whatsoever for the project. However, he got all the credit.

그는 그 프로젝트를 위해 한 게 조금도 없거든. 근데 그가 모든 칭찬은 다 받았어.

☑ whatsoever: 부정문 뒤에서 강조

② work

Whenever I have a headache, I take this pill which is sort of a pain killer. It works really well.

나는 머리가 아플 때마다 진통제 종류인 이 약을 먹어. 정말 효과가 좋아.

☑ work: 일하다, 효과가 좋다

- It works wonders. 효과가 정말 좋아.(=do wonders for+[sb/st])

③ what a relief

A: My dog has returned after missing for two hours.
B: What a relief!

A: 우리 개가 없어진지 두 시간 만에 돌아왔어.
B: 다행이다!

☑ relief 안도

☑ It's a relief+[to+동사원형/that+주어+동사]

Day 362

① **watery**

This batter is too watery. I think I should put more flour.

반죽이 너무 묽어. 밀가루를 더 넣어야겠다.

= liquidy 묽은 ↔ stiff 된

② **weigh**

I'm trying to weigh which one is better for me.

어느 것이 나한테 더 나을지 따져보는 중이야.

☑ weigh: 따져보다, 재보다

weigh the pros and cons: 장단점을 따져보다

③ **worth+[명사/동사ing]**

The museum is definitely worth a visit. You can learn so much about Korean history.

그 박물관은 정말 가볼 만해. 한국역사에 대해 많은 것을 배울 수 있어.

☑ worth+[명사/동사ing]: ~할 만한 가치가 있는

worth [visiting/reading/watching …]

Day 363

① what do you say

What do you say we play badminton?

우리 배드민턴 치는 거 어때?

= Let's play badminton, what do you say?

- How about playing badminton?
- Why don't we play badminton?
- Shall we play badminton?

② While you're at it

While you're at it, could you get me some ice cream?

가는 김에, 아이스크림 좀 사다주라.

☑ While you're at it: ~하는 김에

③ wish

A: Did you see the full moon on 추석?
B: Yes, I wished for my family's health and happiness.

A: 너 추석에 보름달 봤니?
B: 응, 나는 가족들의 건강과 행복을 빌었어.

☑ wish 주어+과거시제

- I wish it [weren't/wasn't] raining. 비가 안 왔으면. (현재 비가 오는 중)
- I wish it hadn't rained. 비가 안 왔었으면 좋았을걸. (과거에 비가 옴)
- I hope it won't rain this weekend. 이번 주말에 비가 안 왔으면 좋겠어.

Day 364

① wrap up

It's already five. Let's wrap it up!

벌써 다섯 시네. 우리 오늘은 여기서 끝내자!

☑ It's a wrap! 끝!

☑ I should wrap up the present I bought today. 나 오늘 산 선물 포장해야 해.

② way+비교급

It's way faster than my previous laptop.

이게 내가 전에 쓰던 노트북보다 훨씬 더 빨라.

☑ way(=much) + 비교급

way better / way more comfortable …

③ without further ado

So, without further ado, let's get to the point.

자, 거두절미하고 요점으로 들어가자.

Day 365

① **you name it**

They sell everything, kitchen utensils, school supplies... you name it!

그곳엔 없는 게 없어, 주방용품, 학용품... 뭐든 다 있어!

☑ you name it: 네가 생각할 수 있는 무엇이든
(어떤 것의 광범위한 다양성을 표현할 때)

② **you can't have your cake and eat it too**

A: Even though I love being in the countryside, I can't stand all these bugs.

B: Well, I guess you can't have your cake and eat it too.

A: 시골에 사는 건 정말 좋은데 이 벌레들은 진짜 질색이야.

B: 뭐, 모든 것을 가질 순 없지.

③ **zip up**

Zip up! It's pretty cold out there.

지퍼 잠가! 밖이 꽤 추워.

☑ button up: 단추 잠가

④ **zone out**(=space out)

People seem to enjoy zoning out while doing nothing. There's even a competition for that.

사람들이 아무것도 안하면서 멍하게 있는 것을 즐기는 듯해. 심지어는 멍때리기 시합도 있어.